MW00652245

Praise for *Go Ask Your Mothers*

"As a Human Resources Leader across major international corporations for more than 30 years, I wholeheartedly endorse this groundbreaking book. Offering invaluable insights and actionable strategies, it serves as an indispensable guide for managers and HR professionals to create a mom-supportive workplace. With a focus on effective communication and advancing support for women in the business realm, this resource is a game changer for fostering inclusivity and elevating the role of mothers in the professional landscape."

—Eriko Talley, retired Senior Vice President of Human Resources, Coca-Cola; former Head of HR, APAC, Facebook; and former Head of HR, Amazon Japan

"Sarah Wells explores the essentials of fostering a thriving workplace by embracing the fundamental elements of human connection and community. Her refreshing perspective as a leader and mom herself provides valuable insights into supporting parents, offering a compelling narrative that vividly captures the experiences of mothers in the workforce. This book is an indispensable guide for creating environments where both employees and managers flourish together. It's a must-read for all working moms and the other women and men who work with and need to better understand them."

—Anthony Silard, Author, *Love and Suffering*; Associate Professor and Director, The Center for Sustainable Leadership, Luiss Business School, Rome; and Distinguished Visiting Professor of Leadership, Monterrey Institute of Technology

"Having spent more than a decade in leadership roles within major law firms, I've grappled with balancing financial objectives, spearheading strategic plans, and cultivating a workplace that thrives on efficiency and inclusivity. Sarah Wells's book provides practical insights for leaders seeking to maintain this equilibrium, particularly by addressing the distinct hurdles that working mothers encounter. It underscores the critical importance of supporting mothers in the workforce, emphasizing how their success is integral to the broader organizational success of the company."

—Lori Brown-Simmons, Executive Director of
Whiteford, Taylor & Preston LLP, and former
Senior Executive at multiple Am Law 100 Firms

"In *Go Ask Your Mothers*, Sarah Wells unveils a guide that resonates deeply with leaders like myself, who are navigating the complexities of team management. This book is a valuable resource for cultivating strong and powerful teams, aligning seamlessly with the principles I hold dear in my own leadership journey."

—Tamara O'Neil, Vice President and
Chief Development Officer at a Leading Nonprofit

GO ASK
YOUR
MOTHERS

GO ASK YOUR MOTHERS

One Simple Step for Managers to Support Working Moms for Team Success

SARAH WELLS

Matt Holt Books
An Imprint of BenBella Books, Inc.
Dallas, TX

Matt Holt is an imprint of BenBella Books, Inc.
10440 N. Central Expressway
Suite 800
Dallas, TX 75231
benbellabooks.com
Send feedback to feedback@benbellabooks.com

BenBella and *Matt Holt* are federally registered trademarks.

Printed in the United States of America
10 9 8 7 6 5 4 3 2 1

Library of Congress Control Number: 2024001109
ISBN 9781637745571 (hardcover)
ISBN 9781637745588 (electronic)

Editing by Lydia Choi
Copyediting by Ginny Glass
Proofreading by Kelly Lenkevich and Becky Maines
Text design and composition by PerfecType, Nashville, TN
Author photo by Emerson Street Photography
Cover design by Morgan Carr
Cover image © Adobe Stock /snesivan
Printed by Lake Book Manufacturing

To the supporter of all my big ideas,
my beloved husband, Greg.

To my daughters, Maddy and Abby, who motivate
me every day to leave the world a better place
for the next generation of working moms.

To all the extraordinary working mothers
in my life, most notably, Kelly Bollinger,
Lizzy Warneck, and Annie Acs.

CONTENTS

CONTENTS

INTRODUCTION

Ten years ago, when I returned to work as a new mom in a leadership position at a nonprofit, I was dog tired and riddled with anxiety about how to speak up for what I needed. "I just have to make it through a year here to prove I didn't leave because of having a baby," I said to my husband on one particularly bad night as I stood in the kitchen washing breast pump parts and wiping tears from my cheeks. "I don't want people to resent hiring me or to avoid hiring moms in the future."

The leaders in my organization were great people, but I didn't want them to see me as less of an employee now that I was a mom. I equated having needs in the workplace with being a failure. And I was worried about what they might be thinking: *It's not the same easy Sarah we liked before. Motherhood is a distraction. She can't manage being both a mom and a professional.* Speaking up, even in the high-level position I was in at the time, felt impossible. I wasn't even sure what to ask for in terms of support. I muddled through those first couple of years. Saw a therapist. Took the flexible work option when I could. Wasn't really in touch with what leadership and colleagues around me *actually* felt about my new self, as I was enmeshed in my own stress of managing it all.

Now, thirteen years later and a mom to two daughters, I'm the CEO of Sarah Wells Breast Pump Bags, a multimillion-dollar company that celebrates working moms. The colorful and fashionable bags and other products I design are a declaration of not hiding or being weighed down by motherhood in the workplace. Instead, they outwardly celebrate motherhood in the professional environment, blending mom life and work life together because both are important. My company has given me a direct connection to tens of thousands of working moms, who have shared their stories, worries, and ideas for improving support in the workplace.

In 2021, I was a guest on the *Express Yourself* mom podcast, where I spoke about my perspective as a company owner and working mom. I said all the right things for the audience of moms, sharing my hacks and tips for transitioning back to work, such as building up a support system and stashing away some breast milk. But when the podcast ended, I realized that my advice felt incomplete. I had only focused on one aspect of the dynamic: the mom's role in making the work experience a successful one. What about those of us who supervise these moms? When people announce their pregnancies, we might celebrate them with an office baby shower, explain their legal rights and company benefits, and wish them well. When they return to the office, however, we hope for the best but often aren't prepared to create the supportive space they need to thrive in our organizations.

A poignant story of misalignment between management, policies, and support for working moms came to me from Amanda, a nurse in a critical care unit in a large hospital system and a new mom. She shared with me that she does get the legally protected breaks to breast pump. But the lactation room, located on the hospital's bottom floor, is a ten-minute walk away from the top floor of the hospital, where she monitors patients. "Even if I could make it there, pump, and get back by some miracle of time, I don't want to be that far from my patients," she said.

Even when we have the best intentions, when we don't engage with working moms for their feedback or, better yet, include them in the design of parent-focused initiatives, we often miss the mark in our management practices. But as you'll see in the success stories I'll share with you throughout this book, opening the conversation with your employees makes space for solutions to flow. For Amanda and her employer, all it might take to resolve this very real problem is a small room for breast pumping near the critical care unit—not necessarily a big or expensive fix. But the silence between employer and mom has negative consequences for all. Later, I'll share the impact this type of silence had on Amanda and her employer.

Over the past three years, I conducted surveys and polls and issued conversation prompts with over one thousand working moms across a variety of professional sectors. Research was conducted in several formats, including an online survey with demographic and open-ended questions, social media polls and open-ended question prompts, and in-depth interviews with mothers willing to share complete stories and anecdotes.

In my online survey, created as a form and sent out to my email list and social media followers, I asked demographic questions regarding the age of children, employment status, professional sector, length of employment, and whether the mom was working remotely, in person, or through a hybrid setup. Further, I probed for work–life satisfaction in a combination of rating-scale responses and open-ended questions, such as the following:

1. Have you ever thought about leaving your job because of lack of support for working moms?
2. How many times has your employer (your boss, HR, anyone in charge of your position) asked how they can support you as a working mom?
3. Do you feel your employer communicates (asks) enough about supporting you as a working mom?

4. If your employer has asked how they can support you as a working mom, tell me more about it: What was this conversation like? How and when did it happen? How did it make you feel that they asked you what you need?

5. Have *you* ever asked your employer for support as a working mom?

Because some working moms are managers themselves, I also assessed supervisory responsibilities for respondents to determine whether manager moms had different responses than supervised moms. Many of the respondents to this extensive survey had additional information to share beyond the online questions and became the subjects of my follow-up interviews, telling their compelling stories shared throughout the chapters of this book.

Social media is a relevant and useful tool for reaching working moms of younger kids. As will be discussed in a later chapter, moms are connecting on more than just pictures of their kids and the latest fashions on social media— social media groups can become their primary community. I have over fifty thousand Instagram followers (89 percent female, 88 percent in the United States, and 95.1 percent aged 18–44) with a high engagement rate, as my brand is trusted among moms not just for products but also as a resource for working moms. Social media presented a unique opportunity for me to issue polls on pertinent topics throughout the development of this book. Oftentimes, I would post the same questions at different times of day or spaced apart by six or twelve months. The results gave me a wide reach of working moms over the years following the COVID-19 pandemic, ensuring that the information now in this book is relevant and not just a small snapshot of one day or week. The types of questions I asked on social media included the following: Do you ask for working-mom support at work when you need it? Do you think the topic of working-mom support should be initiated by managers or employees? Would you leave your current job if your manager didn't initiate conversations about working-mom support? What kinds of support do you wish you had from your manager as a working mom?

Of the moms I researched, 68 percent said their employers do not communicate enough with employees about support, and half of these moms are considering leaving their jobs right now as a result. Read this statistic again and let it sink in.

Let me share some additional statistics that may stun you. They even surprised me, despite knowing through my own firsthand experience that working moms want more communication with managers. More than 50 percent of moms I surveyed for this book had never had any communication with their employer about working-mom support, and an additional 30 percent had only been granted one conversation—most often about parental benefits, usually with human resources, often not even with their direct manager. April, a sales engineer, told me: "I felt as though we are supposed to come back to work almost like nothing happened during our maternity leave and pretend that we aren't feeling lost after being out for weeks and exhausted from caring for our child. If my boss had asked me what I needed, that would have been amazing. Some things may go without saying, but it's still nice to hear it or be told."

Dear managers: it is my firm belief that creating a mom-supportive workplace *is* our competitive advantage and retention survival strategy in a postpandemic job market. Millions of women left the workforce during COVID-19, largely because of the stress of managing the care of children and job demands.[1] Even though those women have begun to return to the job market in the years following the pandemic, without manager support, their long-term success in the workplace is in jeopardy.

The cost of losing valuable team members is a significant hit to our organizations' bottom lines—to the tune of 100 to 200 percent of each employee's annual salary in

1. Matt Gonzales, "Nearly 2 Million Fewer Women in Labor Force," Society for Human Resources Management, February 17, 2022, www.shrm.org/topics-tools/news/inclusion-equity-diversity/nearly-2-million-fewer-women-labor-force.

job replacement costs[2] and $650 billion in working-mother loss for the US economy in the 2020 pandemic year alone, a key part of what was dubbed the "Great Resignation" in the American workforce.[3]

The shift in workplace culture because of the COVID-19 pandemic brought a greater focus on well-being, whole-person, and mental health support in the form of leadership strategies and priorities but virtually no conversation about how to help employers do this in practice with working moms specifically. In this book, I am going to empower you to break the silence with working moms. As CEO of a business geared toward working moms, I have unique access to their voices across many sectors. These moms have a lot to say and are passionate about helping you understand them. With their permission, I'm opening my inbox to you.

I'm aware of the privilege and limitations of my context—I'm a white woman in her forties who has worked

---

2. Chase Charaba, "Employee Retention: The Real Cost of Losing an Employee," *PeopleKeep* (blog), originally published February 2, 2023, last updated September 18, 2023, www.people keep.com/blog/employee-retention-the-real-cost-of-losing-an -employee.

3. Amanda Novello, "The Cost of Inaction: How a Lack of Family Care Policies Burdens the U.S. Economy and Families," July 2021, National Partnership for Women and Families, www.national partnership.org/our-work/resources/economic-justice/other/cost -of-inaction-lack-of-family-care-burdens-families.pdf.

in several job sectors, with moms on my teams mostly in midlevel or higher professional roles. Your context is likely different. You might be a law firm partner working with associates with advanced degrees and some longevity in their careers. You might be a gym manager and with moms working part-time on hourly wages. You might be a hospital administrator overseeing night shift health-care-worker moms who have unique challenges that don't align with standard childcare options. Cultural, familial, racial, economic, industry, and other differences impact moms and organizations in vastly different ways. We each bring our own unique experiences and perspectives, some more privileged than others. However, there is one action that all managers can take that will improve outcomes for their organizations: talking with all moms to create a plan that establishes support for a successful transition back to work.

Now more than ever, we cannot afford to lose these highly valuable employees. Working moms are an essential and growing part of our teams from entry level to executive. Working mothers of young children are in no way an anomaly these days; by age forty-four, 85 percent of American women will be mothers.[4] Labor force participation for

---

4. Claire Miller, "The U.S. Fertility Rate Is Down, Yet More Women Are Mothers," *New York Times*, January 18, 2018, www .nytimes.com/2018/01/18/upshot/the-us-fertility-rate-is-down-yet -more-women-are-mothers.html.

moms is on the rise, with over 75 percent employed, and nearly 70 percent of moms who have young kids under the age of six are working.[5] Losing moms is costly for our organizations in terms of turnover and depletion of institutional knowledge and skills and hurts team morale. Like many of you, I have experienced turnover among mom employees, feeling frustrated when they leave even when I thought I was doing all the right things. I know firsthand how hard it is taking the time and energy to manage teams in a way that builds morale and addresses well-being in the workplace. But the costs of losing these moms is greater.

Moms do bear responsibility to navigate their new world—and trust me when I tell you, from being there myself, that they are trying hard to figure this out in networking groups, from mom classes, with their partners, and in therapy. To put things in perspective, moms working full-time are spending the better part of their lives in our workplaces or on our Zoom calls. Doing some quick math, we discover there will never be a literal balance between work and motherhood: full-time work will always win on hours. In a typical workweek, a full-time employed mom will be with us on the job forty—or a lot more—hours and perhaps fifteen or twenty with her awake child or children. But figuring out how to be a mom and a successful

5. "Employment Characteristics of Families—2022," US Department of Labor, April 19, 2023, www.bls.gov/news.release/pdf/famee.pdf.

employee is *not* the sole responsibility of moms; while powerful in other ways, they are not the power holders in the manager–mom relationship. We managers hold the key to flexible schedules and well-being initiatives—and the location of lactation rooms.

In my years of listening to working moms, the key thing they say they want is to be heard or seen by their employers. They want to know that we understand that when they come back to the workplace, they are changed. They want us to realize that there are new, sweeping logistical, social, emotional, and professional needs on their part. They want to be included in decision-making about parenting benefits and policies, and they want to know that our teams are a safe place for conversations about struggle and support.

There will always be moms who do not come back from leave for reasons outside of our control, like shifting priorities, moving across the country, or having a career change of heart. But we're not talking here about the normal course of turnover; we're talking about moms leaving our organizations because they are unsupported. We're talking about a real opportunity for us to improve team outcomes. The evidence shows that if we don't ask about support, working moms then think we don't care about their changed situation. It would be a shame to assume these moms are going to leave us anyway, while they assume we don't care, when all along we could make a difference together.

Support for Other Parents

This book has been written for the explicit support of working moms. I chose to focus on working moms as opposed to all parents as one group because I think there are unique issues, challenges, and supports needed for moms that get lost in broader conversations of workplace well-being, family support, and policies. I will go into those specific topics, such as breastfeeding and mental health, in great detail in the chapters to come. But let me also say this: all working parents need support, and the strategies for managers to communicate with their teams in this book can be applied to any parent or any worker juggling career and caregiving. I have watched my husband work through the transition of becoming a working father, needing time and support to make the transition into parenthood and having to make those this-or-that choices daily, well beyond when our girls were babies. Whether you manage moms, dads, partners, birthing parents, or caregivers of a grandparent or other family members, your ability to be a supportive manager is critical to their success on your team.

Supporting working moms creates positive team environments where all challenges, whether or not they relate to parenting, will be more effectively met. Mental health was a critical issue brought forth in nearly every one of the mom stories I heard throughout my research for this book. Mental health challenges are inevitably present in all demographics on your team, so bringing them out into the open for the sake of working mothers, strengthening your communication and resources for mental health support or similar topics, will then benefit every type of team member you ever hire. As a manager, consider how you can utilize some of the teachings in this book to dive in deeper with other parents and nonparents on your team and really know who they are and what they need to be wildly successful for your team and organization.

Support Through the Continuum of Parenting

It is critical to provide support to working moms throughout the continuum of parenting. This book is focused on mothers who have recently made the transition to parenthood and who are navigating their new lives at home and at work. However, the desire to be there for your child and the support needed from managers doesn't stop for a mom who is finally sleeping through the night or who has sent their child off to elementary school. While moms gain experience along the way and develop coping strategies and routines for success at work, there is a continued need for schedule flexibility; empathy when parenting is tough during illness, conflict, divorce, death, transitions between major child-developmental stages, or the birth or adoption of subsequent children; and anything else that may crop up for working mothers along a lifetime of parenting responsibilities.

When you make a new hire of a working mom with older children, or as the working moms on your team stay and their kids grow up, managers must remain committed to the supportive approaches shared within these chapters. Moms of older kids might have fewer evident support needs and be able to put in longer hours than moms with young kids, but they still appreciate flexibility to check in on their sick teenager at home or to participate in milestone events at school. While your working moms might move beyond the stage of a baby waking them at night, managers should be aware that these moms might still be losing sleep over academic, social, financial, or mental health concerns in parenting older children; they all still need your support. In this book, I'm talking about new moms—those who have babies and toddlers and young elementary-age kids, who are at the start of their motherhood journey. But the need for support continues throughout all of parenthood.

Support Is Not Performance Based

Keep in mind throughout this book that while it may be easy to communicate with and provide support to the working moms on your team you already think highly of because of strong performance, support is not earned by performance. I will provide you with evidence in statistics and stories that employee support begets strong performance and retention. You may even find that a new mom who was previously lagging in some areas on the job will bring new enthusiasm and skills to the table from the experience of motherhood when your workplace is properly supportive.

Organizations honor all major policies or accommodations to their employees regardless of performance; the same must be true of working-mom support. As managers, we must make decisions about employee performance and ongoing job status separate from our willingness and efforts to provide support. Support of working moms is not earned as a reward; it is a critical part of good management practice to maximize the potential of your employees.

Leave Policies Are Fundamental, But Just One Piece of the Puzzle

Paid family leave may be at the top of the list of what your team members bring to you as needed support, and you should do all in your power to make it happen. Paid leave is a critical factor in keeping women in the workforce and economically secure and in supporting maternal and mental health. Paid leave is also critical in promoting breastfeeding, which has been shown to improve the health outcomes for moms and babies, saving employers money in their insurance programs and retaining valuable employees in their jobs.[6] However, my intention throughout this book is to think bigger and broader than paid leave alone as the solution to supporting working moms. Paid leave is an important piece of the puzzle for working mothers and other parents; however, based on the moms I have interacted with over the last decade in my professional capacity and through my own experience as a new mom, I have found that when the support-for-moms topic centers exclusively around leave, it can create a perception that support only happens upon passage of a federal leave policy. I do not believe this is the case at all. Support is for now, important policies in place or not.

I talked with Brooke, a customer located in Canada, about this issue of paid leave and how that plays out for support of working moms in her organization. I was particularly interested to hear a perspective from outside the United States, from someone in a country that already has a federal policy mandating leave. Brooke, a psychiatric nurse, was provided up to eighteen months of paid-leave benefits. When I asked her whether she considers her job a supportive workplace of mothers, she had mixed feelings:

6. Kathleen Romig and Kathleen Bryant, "A National Paid Leave Program Would Help Workers, Families," Center for Budget and Policy Priorities, April 27, 2021, www.cbpp.org/research/economy /a-national-paid-leave-program-would-help-workers-families.

I believe that even with paid maternity wage, employers are not always supportive of working moms. I felt like my employer believes absolutely everything about new motherhood, including breastfeeding, figuring out childcare, and so forth, should be done by the end of the paid leave. Interestingly, it is almost like, because of the paid-leave benefit, they do not believe they have to accommodate anything more after I come back to work. The problem with that is that you are still a mom of a young kid a year after giving birth, and you still need support. You might still be breastfeeding. And your kids still get sick. You still must work logistics of childcare. You are still tired.

I think if my manager had been more open with me while I was pregnant, I may have been able to stay on the job until I gave birth rather than take an early leave. I was having problems with safety on the job, and there was not a way I felt comfortable talking to my manager about my concerns. I think my manager figured that since she had submitted the required paperwork for my leave, her job in supporting me was done.

The lack of conversation between me and my manager before going on leave leads me to believe it will be more of the same noncommunication when I return, and I am actively seeking a different job right now for when my leave concludes.

Please give your working moms the very best maternity leave you can possibly provide. I know as a small business how hard this is; I recently offered three-month paid
maternity leave to someone on my team for the first time.
It took me ten years to get a point where I had the funds to
cover that cost and a large enough team to cover the workload. And it was still hard as a manager to overcome the
workload gap in this employee being out, but I am here to
tell you firsthand that it was one of my proudest achieve-
ments in business. But even with an important and robust
leave policy, with or without a federal requirement behind
it, you need to create a workplace that is supportive well
beyond leave. Combining the two—great parental-leave
policies with excellent ongoing support—will pay off in
creating a supportive work culture for moms and other
new parents.

Recently, I experienced this with my team. As one
of my team members was nearing the nine-week mark
of her twelve weeks out of the office on maternity leave,
she asked to return early in a part-time capacity. "Are you
sure you want to return? I want to protect this important time we have given you," I said, thinking I was doing
the right thing. She was adamant. "I'm not ready to be
back full-time until the twelve weeks are up, but I want
to dip my toe back in and help you out. I'm excited about
returning to work and getting back to the job that I love,

and I feel so supported that it's not scary to return." I was certainly happy to welcome her expertise back in the fold. What a surprise!

You should not expect that working mothers will want to shorten their leave; clearly, that is not the point I am making here, and please do not ask them to do so. I do not expect the next new mom on my team that goes out on leave to end their time off early, nor would I judge them for taking their full leave. The point is this: my team member and I have been closely communicating through her fertility journey, pregnancy, delivery, NICU experience, and maternity leave. And because she had a clear transition plan and organization-wide support for her needs, she felt ready to be back before we were even planning on it. It's a testament to the power of feeling so wholly supported that you feel you can have it all—the job you love and the baby in your arms. My team member felt the support she needed to make the choices about work and parenting life that were best for her. I am so proud of our strong communicative partnership. I know the supportive environment I have created will result in better outcomes for my team member, and it is better for my business to retain this highly skilled and trained individual.

Paid leave is critical and should be made available whenever possible. Effective and frequent communication to get a plan in place for management to support the continuum of the working mom experience *after* moms return from leave is also essential.

––––––––––

My intention in this book is not to shame or scold you for your approach with moms nor provide a generic script to use with these employees. This book is also not a template for a benefits review nor a human resources manual, though it is about making powerful and lasting human connections. If you are a new manager, this book will show you how to take the first steps to create a culture of support for working moms. And even if you are already a champion for working moms, this book will help you take your approach to the next level. For all of us managers, there is work to be done because relationships need work continuously. This book will empower you to have open, informed conversations with the working moms on your teams to produce positive results for both the organization and the mom. My goal is to equip you with the simple yet powerful insight I have gained directly from my employees and customers, which these moms say can make the difference between their staying at or leaving your organization, between success or struggle on the job. The goal of this book is to start a conversation between manager and working mom, organization and employees, and management and mom communities. I will help you pinpoint exactly how you are going to start—or build on—your support of working moms.

In the first chapter of the book, I open with stories from working moms to provide you with insider knowledge of what they say they want and need from their managers. In chapter two, I'll equip you with the business case for retaining working moms for short- and long-term savings and explain how these employees' unique skills and perspectives bring bottom-line value to your organization. Next, in chapter three, I'll examine what I've heard from my manager and leader colleagues over the years on why we might hesitate as managers to initiate conversations about support with working moms. I'll take a deep dive in chapter four on why moms aren't asking *you* for what they need, particularly because of the intense societal pressure and scrutiny they face while returning to work. By learning about the tension that exists between organizations and working moms, you'll have the understanding to create—or enhance—empathy that will enable communication, which I'll emphasize as the most critical tool for a successful manager/working mom relationship in chapter five. To equip you to jump on this opportunity to improve your organization, I've developed a robust road map in chapter six to initiate conversations with the moms on your teams to develop an environment of support. We'll close in chapter seven with a great success story that will help you see how these steps are easily within reach for managers in many types of organizations and visualize how the ultimate sustainable support for working moms might look like in your organization.

Lauren, a physician mom, messaged me one day to say that support from her manager began at the start of her pregnancy. "My boss would routinely check in with me. And now as I'm preparing to return in one week, I have had several informal text check-ins and formal email check-ins to discuss pumping routines and optimizing my clinic and surgical schedule for motherhood. I feel so lucky and happy about returning to my job." And Erin, an administrative assistant in a large nonprofit organization, told me: "My direct supervisor showed so much care upon my return to work after baby that I was comfortable asking for what I needed. If they hadn't done that, I probably would have been silent because we are conditioned to think that pregnancy is a hindrance to job performance. Compassionate leadership is a priority in where I choose to work." As managers, this kind of excitement and satisfaction for the job is what we aspire to for our teams; we know that motivated employees stick around and work hard for the mission.

By the end of this book, you'll be eager to schedule a call or meeting with a working mom like Lauren's boss did. You'll discover how good *you* feel when you see how much working moms appreciate an empathetic boss. And your company will save money through retention while reaping the benefits of some of the best employees you can recruit: moms. You *can* be a supportive manager and create an organization where working moms want to stay and excel. This is an investment worth making for the success of your teams. I'll help you get there. Let's go!

1

What Working Moms Say After Hours About Management

When even the night owls have gone to sleep, moms are up breastfeeding, calming a nightmare, shushing a colicky baby. After being jolted out of their good-while-it-lasted attempt at sleep, they go online seeking community—studies show that most American moms, as high as 88 percent, use multiple social media platforms: more than half access them daily, and three-quarters are utilizing these platforms to build community and find

GO ASK YOUR MOTHERS

support.[1] My own kids are past the baby stage, but as the owner of a company that creates and facilitates community for new moms, I too am up in the wee hours talking to moms about the pressing issues on their minds. When my phone vibrates on my nightstand with the latest direct message, I often find moms feeling profoundly unheard, misunderstood, or neglected at their jobs. To avoid seeming burdensome, these moms frequently preface their worries with "I know I'm lucky to have this good job, but . . ." or "I chose to be a working mom, but . . ." Over the eleven years I have been talking with these moms, I have learned that the so-called Sunday scaries—the anxiety on the eve of the start to the work week—quickly becomes the five-night fright for a mom who feels they must navigate the transition back to work flawlessly, a constant wear-and-tear on their mental health.

Moms tell me that their managers often ask to see a baby photo or share a brief welcome-back email on the day of their return, but they are not asked in a substantive and meaningful way about their transition back to work, let

1. Molly E. Waring, Loneke T. Blackman Carr, and Grace E. Heerspring, "Social Media Use Among Parents and Women of Childbearing Age in the US," Centers for Disease Control and Prevention, February 16, 2023, dx.doi.org/10.5888/pcd20.220194; Maeve Duggan, Amanda Lenhart, Cliff Lampe, and Nicole B. Ellison, "Parents and Social Media," Pew Research Center, July 16, 2015, www.pewresearch.org/internet/2015/07/16/parents-and-social -media/.

26

alone how things are going months or years later. Here's a story from Elise, one of the frontline heroes we most value in our communities:

I go to work each day as a nurse in an ICU to save lives. I'm motivated to be there and passionate about my work. I miss my kids terribly while I work, but I see the big picture impact of the work that I do. But I don't feel valued or heard by management.

I wish my boss asked me questions like: What shifts would work best with my childcare availability? How am I feeling back on this intense job now that I have a small child at home? Or: What kind of accommodations do I need for breast pumping?

During the [COVID-19] pandemic, we did not have adequate PPE to keep ourselves safe, therefore not keeping our little ones safe. Work and home are interrelated in many ways, sometimes in matters of life or death. We moms are expected to acknowledge and navigate that, but it feels like management has a part in trying to navigate this, too.

If our hospital leadership had asked me more about how I was feeling about work and family, if they had given me the support I needed, and if they had made sure coworkers understood existing policies, I would have felt supported. But I don't feel supported, and I am planning to leave this job.

For Elise and other moms, work and family are insep-
arable. The so-called work–life balance aspirational goal
for employees is built on the notion that these components
of life are important but separate. The happiest working
moms tell me the goal is satisfactory work–life *blend*, not
balance. The two components of life are always mixing—the
late-night client email responded to from bed or the unexpected sick-child support that conflicts with a meeting, and
so on—and one or the other takes priority in unplanned
and unequal ways. If an employer insists on compartmen-
talizing work from family, and either actively or passively
ignores the mixture of the personal with the professional,
moms say the blend goes sour quickly.

When I conducted my survey of working moms, 53 percent said they were never asked anything about their transition back to work, and an additional 25 percent said the single
conversation they had with their manager was brief or policy-
oriented only. *Three-quarters of the moms I talked to said
their communication with managers about working-mom
support was seriously lacking or nonexistent.* What moms
tell me is simple and obvious but not happening: they wish
their managers would ask them how they are doing and what
they need at work to navigate the transition and be successful
in the jobs they care deeply about. They would like communication with their managers, initiated by their managers.

The United States is woefully behind on paid leave,
affordable childcare, and other family support; we are in dire

need of better public policies. But a manager should not wait for an act of Congress to do something about employee support. Right now, you can make a significant difference for new moms on your team. You can start communicating with your working moms today; it's as simple as scheduling a Zoom meeting or sending a text. You might be thinking, *That's it? I just initiate a conversation?* Yes, working moms want you to ask how they are doing and how you can support them. In chapter six, I'll share best practices and specific tips on how to carry out these conversations, as well as several powerful success stories. In chapters two and three, I will dissect and expose the reasons many managers and moms are still struggling to develop effective communication together.

The stress of poor or insufficient communication and support of working moms has undesirable consequences. For organizations, losing working moms costs time and money, negatively affects organizational and team performance, and contributes to a growing labor gap, which is particularly striking in the most in-demand careers where younger women tend to dominate, such as health care and retail sales.[2] Moms often share with me that as the pressures of work and family mount, they begin forming an exit

---

2. Greg Lewis and Manas Mohapatra, "The Most In-Demand Jobs on LinkedIn Right Now," LinkedIn.com, accessed November 2, 2023, www.linkedin.com/business/talent/blog/talent-strategy/most-in-demand-jobs.

plan in their mind. They start looking at other job openings, talk with friends about possible career shifts, and begin to check out of their passion for the job. In my survey, more than 50 percent of working moms were thinking about leaving their job because of lack of support, and nearly 10 percent—most of whom were in just the first months or years of parenting—had already moved on from one employer to another. Some of the moms I talked to quit their jobs during our conversations for this book.

A stereotype still exists that working moms are fixated on finding a way to stay home with baby. This is always a choice we should respect but is not the case for the majority of moms in this country, by choice or necessity. When I talk to moms, most are devastated and unsettled about having to change jobs to find a supportive environment. Moms like Maria, an information-management specialist, care deeply about their work. "I just wish my manager and I had an open conversation about how I felt about stepping away from my job during maternity leave," Maria told me. "I am more nervous to leave my job duties in someone else's hands than I am worried about giving birth. I care about my position, which I have put a lot of effort into building up at our company."

And for Amanda, the critical care nurse whose story I shared in the introduction, the lack of logistical support for breastfeeding when she returned to her job impacted her job satisfaction, which had negative consequences for her and her employer just a few months after our first conversation:

> *It was an extremely difficult decision, but I have left my job. The lack of support for breastfeeding was terrible. But the straw that broke the camel's back is that I received a mediocre annual review after working diligently and with dedication through the pressures of a pandemic. I was cited for having been on leave of absence for ten weeks, which they say created an incomplete picture of my performance.*
>
> *It wasn't easy to quit, but breastfeeding was just the start of the support I would need as a mom at work, and I knew I had to make a change for the long term.*
>
> *I'm now training at a different hospital to be a labor-and-delivery nurse. Immediately, there was a 180-degree shift in support. There is a pumping space in the unit itself, and the management is very supportive of my needs as a working mom. Moving to a new hospital, and a different unit, where the culture has a radically different approach to supporting moms, is an astounding and life-changing experience.*

It goes without saying that family is a priority, and some moms want to or need to be home full-time with their child or children, but don't discount how many want to be at their jobs and need to do well there. Leaving jobs has major consequences for mothers as well as employers: it can result in loss of income or a step back in career. In some cases, it can involve a new investment of significant time and energy—or retraining, like in Amanda's case—to overcome learning curves, may require reworking childcare plans, and may result in less stability while building back up paid time off and reputation with management and colleagues.

Moms worry about how to be good moms while at work. And moms worry about their career success while at home. Many working moms have invested significant time and money in their education and training. They often care about career advancement, quality performance, and maintaining an income in a workplace where they have longevity. When the moms I talk with decide to leave their jobs, the decision does not come lightly. It often comes down to a lack of communication and support, a deal-breaker for many because it directly impacts their ability to get support not only as a mother but also as an employee.

Mental Health

Nothing quite gets my conversations rolling with working moms like the topic of mental health. Every time I ask on my social media platforms, "How is your mental health, working mamas?" thousands of moms engage. The conversation about mental health can be profound and frightening: many working moms are *not* doing okay. Since I started writing this book, the percent of moms suffering with postpartum depression (PPD) has gone up; where I was once finding research stating 10 percent, 12.5 percent, maybe 15 percent of women with PPD, the latest research says that in an average year, 20 percent of moms have PPD.[3] Additional studies demonstrate the number as high as 33 percent of new moms suffering with PPD during the COVID-19 pandemic.[4] In other words, *you are likely to have depressed new moms on your teams.*

Symptoms of depression during pregnancy and the period after birth can manifest in a number of ways, as outlined by Postpartum Support International (PSI) in this list:

- Feelings of anger or irritability
- Lack of interest in the baby
- Appetite and sleep disturbance
- Crying and sadness
- Feelings of guilt, shame, or hopelessness

---

3. "Depression During Pregnancy and Postpartum," Postpartum Support International, accessed August 18, 2023, www.postpartum .net/learn-more/depression/.

4. Beata Mostafavi and Laura Bailey, "A Third of New Moms Had Postpartum Depression during Early COVID," University of Michigan: Michigan Medicine, March 23, 2022, www.michigan medicine.org/health-lab/third-new-moms-had-postpartum -depression-during-early-covid.

- Loss of interest, joy, or pleasure in things you used to enjoy
- Possible thoughts of harming the baby or yourself[5]

Interestingly for managers, PSI also states that mothers are at increased risk for PPD and other mental health challenges if they are under significant financial stress, lack adequate childcare support or other kinds of support with baby, have utilized fertility treatments to get pregnant, or had any kind of complications during their new-mom journey, including breastfeeding stress. Further, another study found that mothers with less than twelve weeks of maternity leave at their jobs were at increased risk for PPD due to the lack of time to focus on physical and mental well-being before returning to their job.[6]

Other effects of PPD on moms include a lack of focus and concentration, physical illness, alcohol and drug abuse, relationship problems, suicidal ideations, job loss, and homelessness. Studies show that infants of mothers with PPD also suffer negative outcomes, including being more at safety risk from lack of car seat usage or other important

---

5. "Depression During Pregnancy and Postpartum," Postpartum Support International.

6. Katelin R. Kornfeind and Heather L. Sipsma, "Exploring the Link Between Maternity Leave and Postpartum Depression," *Women's Health Issues* 28, no. 4 (July/August 2018): 321–26, doi.org10 .1016/j.whi.2018.03.008.

safety measures for young children, slower language development, impaired cognitive and motor development, and more.[7] These facts have significant implications for even small-to-midsize organizations, from retention to healthcare costs to employee and team morale.

Many of the moms I spoke with were working to keep their mental health challenges under wraps, away from their employers; the problem with this is that most people cannot compartmentalize or hide untreated, unsupported mental health challenges while at work. Anxiety, depression, and stress compound over time and can boil over in a serious way without an outlet or safe space to receive help. Patricia, a technical designer in the fashion industry, shared her story with me:

> *When I returned to work after ten weeks of maternity leave, my manager and coworkers were welcoming and made sure to check in on me, but the question was always "How's the baby?" and never "How are you really doing?" The pressure to catch up on my workload was intense, but that's not even what caught me off guard. No one warned me that your personal life— this new role of "mom"—would bleed into my work life.*

---

7. Justine Slomian, Germain Honvo, Patrick Emonts, et al., "Consequences of Maternal Postpartum Depression: A Systematic Review of Maternal and Infant Outcomes," *Women's Health* 15, no. 1 (April 2019): 1–55, doi.org/10.1177/1745506519844044.

I couldn't neatly compartmentalize my roles so that when I was at work I was only thinking of and doing work-related things.

My baby was always on my mind: Will he be okay without me? I had to pump frequently, which is almost another job. I'd rush into meetings late after pumping sessions because I had been crying in the mother's room, shirt soaked with milk and eyes red and puffy. I used to be so good with change and transition—after all, that was part of my job in corporate America—so why couldn't I cope with the change of being a working mom?

I thought I was successfully hiding how awful I felt, until one day, about four months postpartum, I snapped and had a full panic attack in the office in front of all my coworkers.

I ended up in the emergency room to make sure I wasn't having a heart attack and was absolutely mortified to go back into the office and face my manager and coworkers.

I wish my manager had checked in earlier, before the panic attack, to ask, "How are you coping with being a working mom?" I wish I had resources through my employer-provided insurance to be screened for postpartum anxiety and depression instead of having to seek treatment myself. I wish I had a peer group of other working parents to ask questions and get advice.

*With these resources, guidance, and support, I would
have transitioned back to work a more confident and,
more importantly, mentally healthy employee.*

Patricia's story sends a strong message to all of us in
management roles: we should *assume* we need to ask working moms about their mental health. Here's something for
you to stew on: for the next decade, women in the workforce
with young kids, or who are starting families soon, will have
been on their working-mom journey during the COVID-19
pandemic. They will have had pregnancy checkups over
telehealth, birthed babies while wearing face masks, sent
toddlers to daycare before a vaccine was available, and
facilitated preschool learning online. They will have had
to find a way to maintain their jobs with this totally new,
uncharted—and scary—experience that continues today
and will shape their entire generation. These moms will
bring resilience and skills to your organization. They will
also bring their anxiety to work.

Working-mom worry and guilt existed before the pandemic, and it will likely continue long after: *Am I a terrible
mom for putting my kid in daycare? Why does it seem like
everyone else is doing this better than I am? Everyone at
work must resent me and think I'm needy.* The usual course
of working-mom worry will be heightened for new and
experienced moms for years to come by trying to transition
to work flawlessly while carrying the weight and logistics of

navigating a global crisis at the very moment they launched into working-mom orbit.

The people who know our day-to-day actions and behaviors the best can most often sense when something is off or prompt us to get help if we need it. That's why you as a manager have a role in mental health check-ins for working moms. Early in the COVID-19 pandemic, I learned this myself. While I was swallowed up by my own parenting, panicking about company sales, and facing exhaustion, I woke up one day and realized I hadn't asked my team how *they* were coping—and I spend the bulk of my week with these folks. When I reached out, the message was the same across the board: we're struggling big-time with our mental health. I offered to pay for virtual therapy for my team. It didn't cost my company much. Some of my team took me up on it, and others did not. But all were incredibly appreciative of the conversation, and there was a notable shift in morale afterward. One of the moms later revealed to me that she was in an extremely dark place—requiring professional intervention—and that my efforts had made a difference in her getting help. And the mom who made a point of telling me how much it meant to have this support continues to work with me; she even took on more responsibility for my company. Supporting mental health needs is a requirement of a good manager: it helps your employees' performance, and it can save lives.

Flexible Scheduling

Moms tell me all the time how they live in a maddening state of frustration because they are a hair shy of the flexible scheduling that they need from their bosses to make it work for their job and children. They perpetually worry about getting kids picked up on time from childcare or how to manage a sick baby who needs to stay home. Most often, the incidents I hear about are systemic smaller problems that add up over time to an enormous amount of stress. For instance, I polled moms about taking care of sick kids—which can feel like a full-time job in the first years as children build up their immune systems. Eighty percent of these moms said they wished they had more flexibility or flex time at work to support their kids when sick. This is a great example because there is not a single working family that escapes having sick children; it's common, frequent, and consistent in every parenting experience. This is a topic for managers to address head-on with all the working moms on their teams: How will we juggle the inevitable winter season of illness with work? You know as a manager that the illnesses are coming; get ahead of them with a conversation and some creative solutions, like a plan for remote work or pooled time off that parents can share with each other. I experienced this shared PTO setup at another organization I worked for, and it was marvelous; parents of older kids who were sick less often could "donate" a couple paid sick days to another parent and pass it along. Think of the morale boost to everyone when you set up plans for support like this.

When I listen to these moms struggling with lack of flexibility, my problem-solving brain instantly starts wondering: *Could your manager flex your hours by thirty minutes? What if they offered Zoom as a backup meeting plan for urgent situations at home? Could the boss chat on speakerphone during the commute to daycare instead of holding you in person at the office? What if you could work longer hours four days a week to get out earlier on Friday for your kiddos' appointments? Kids often go to bed earlier than adults—could your manager allow you to leave an hour early but finish out an hour later at night? Would your team benefit from a desk in the lactation room so they could work during pumping sessions, if they so choose?*

Prior to the start of the COVID-19 pandemic, it may have been more difficult to imagine how to implement some of the changes I have brainstormed here. But now that we have been under tremendous pressure to implement flexible workplaces in a time of crisis and have done so with much success in a lot of our organizations, we see evidence that we can be creative in these ways. It is doable for most managers to reexamine the way they used to do things and come up with flexibilities that best serve employees and thus create better—and more successful—places to work.

Moms have an amazing capacity for workload and efficiency—just ask anyone who's taken a conference call on speaker while driving their car while using a breast pump—and are ready to find a creative solution with you. And it will pay off for your teams to offer all sorts of flexibility, since "for women with child caregiving responsibilities who have remote-work access, the probability of being likely to look for another job in the next year decreases by 32% . . . compared to women with child caregiving responsibilities without remote-work access."[8]

Many working moms have found stopgaps on their own, only to have their strategies fall apart when something goes a bit off plan. Here's an example of this struggle:

> *I work at a bank, and we close around 5 PM. Every day, I sit at my desk at 4:45 PM with growing anxiety. You see, the limited daycare centers in our very small town all close at 5 PM. If you don't pick up your child on time, you face late fees or have to make arrangements for someone else to pick them up.*
>
> *I sit there at the end of the day with extreme pressure building up. I'm anxious and worried, my palms are sweaty, and it's hard to concentrate on the final tasks of the day. How do I finish this day strong but*

8. Tara Van Bommel, "Boost Productivity with Remote-Work Options," Catalyst, 2021, accessed January 2, 2024, www.catalyst .org/reports/remote-work-burnout-productivity/.

get my kid out on time? What's the plan today? Am I being judged by the daycare as a bad mom for not being on time? Are my boss and coworkers annoyed that I'm obviously hustling to get out of here?

I really like my job a lot—I'd even say I'm happy being there. But this logistical issue of the last fifteen or thirty minutes of every single day makes me feel like I've gone into a battle of work versus motherhood. And I cannot win for either. It's a terrible feeling to end every day with this stress. I'm exhausted. I'm starting to resent the job.

I really believe that simple conversations with my employer and a willingness to make slight changes to my schedule would relieve a lot of the burden on me at work and home. But I don't know how to approach them, and they don't approach me, even though I think they know this is an issue for working parents here.

Moms understand that an organization's plans and goals change. But they want a chance to talk with you about any impact on their work schedule, with ample time to address childcare, commute, or workplace location and flexibility, or all three. Erika, who works in procurement in a manufacturing plant, shared with me:

I was a work-from-home employee. Some of our office positions require work on-site, while others, like mine, can be done fully remote. When I came back from leave, I set up childcare in a way that worked for this arrangement and was off and running having a smooth return-to-work experience, as planned and promised.

Unfortunately, other employees who had to work on-site got increasingly upset and frustrated that some employees were working remotely. Without any discussion with employees, leadership decided the best solution was to establish a one-size-fits-all approach and make everyone come back on-site.

I remember that call. I was having a sandwich on a Friday afternoon as I finished up the final tasks for what had been a great and productive week. My boss called and told me about the sudden policy change and let me know I had to be back on-site, full-time, beginning Monday morning. There was no further opportunity for discussion or planning.

I had just a few hours to scramble a plan to make it happen. My current childcare wasn't compatible with the new location and schedule, and I was still sitting on a waitlist—from three months before my baby's birth—for a daycare that would be able to accommodate this location. I ended up suddenly putting my baby in a daycare center I hadn't fully researched, thus didn't fully trust, which caused me a lot of stress. It was also pretty far away, doubling my commute time.

I feel very jaded about it all and unsupported by my company. When I returned from maternity leave, my boss and coworkers wanted to see photos of my baby, melted over my baby's Halloween costume, [and] asked how baby was sleeping, but when I really needed interest and support as a working mom, they didn't ask. I'm looking for a new job.

I know it's hard as a manager to be the bearer of bad news. Letting people down, like not being able to accommodate flexible scheduling, is a bummer part of management. I have experienced this firsthand running my company. One particularly painful time was when I made a new hire in mid-March 2020 and had to call her up right before her start date and say, "I'm sorry. It's now a pandemic, and I just cannot follow through on the job offer." It was awful. I knew it was a terrible time to be out on the market, and perhaps she had already turned down another role elsewhere for mine. It likely impacted her negatively on a personal level, and I'm sorry for that. And there were some real pivots in my past management roles, too. I led a nonprofit through a recession, during which the organization had to make difficult cuts and offer fewer benefits. I also managed an association solely focused on travel-based events through the tragedy and horror of 9/11, which meant cancellations, broken promises, and slowing growth for the team. As I said, being the bearer of bad news is never fun, and sometimes it is unavoidable. But as a manager, it is easier to help your employees understand the reasons behind what you can and cannot do for your team when you have a strong line of communication established.

Childcare

A staggering 51 percent of parents in the United States live in what is known as a "childcare desert," meaning that no reliable or affordable childcare is within reasonable distance of the workplace.[9] Childcare deserts can be a financial *and* a geographic problem, as moms shared in my interviews. They are often found in low-income communities. But these deserts are also found in densely populated urban areas, where a lot of offices are located and the waitlists for childcare can be upward of months or *years* because services cannot meet population growth and subsequent demand, which creates gaps in care for families with all levels of income. Your working moms may have to leave because their job isn't flexing or financially in line with the available childcare, or because the geographic distance between worksite and care center is too great.

9. "51 Percent of People in the United States Live in a Child Care Desert," Center for American Progress, 2018, accessed January 2, 2024, childcaredeserts.org/2018/.

While you as manager may not be able to resolve the childcare desert in your community, you can offer several related supports to retain your employees: higher pay, remote work, flexible hours, on-site childcare, backup childcare, and even connecting employee parents together for shared childcare options. For instance, nanny-share arrangements between employees who live close to each other could split the costs—this is something coworker moms in urban areas often utilize—or you could connect parents on your team so they can utilize the same childcare facilities and share transportation to cut down on travel times.

The moms I talk to say that even a little bit of flexibility goes a long way. For example, providing the option to modify the typical nine-to-five work schedule to 8 AM to 4 PM or 10 AM to 6 PM can help your working moms share the daycare commute with a partner. Or, if a mom remains on a waitlist for the most compatible childcare option for an extra month after leave, allow them to enlist other temporary support, such as working from home with a neighbor or family member providing some help until they can get into an ideal situation. If you can go big on your offer of support, consider setting up on-site childcare services or providing coverage for backup childcare. But at a minimum, talk with your working moms about the childcare situation in your area and how you might alleviate the problems.

The research has shown time and time again that addressing childcare support makes for happier employees:

"83 percent [of mothers] reported that childcare benefits would be an important factor in deciding whether to stay with their current employer or look to switch employers."[10] Supporting a successful interplay between work and childcare for your employees is a clear path toward working-mom retention. What you can offer may not be much, but moms want an opportunity to at least talk about these situations. They want to feel heard and have the chance to propose creative solutions. Maybe you *could* offer a different shift, change a schedule's start or end time, or use your weight in the community to talk with leaders about available childcare services. Maybe all you can offer is an ear as an empathetic listener. The moms tell me that just being heard makes a difference in how they feel about the job. As managers, our best step forward is to ask working mothers what they need and find a path to provide the supports that address those needs.

Support from Coworkers

Moms who are struggling with workplace support tell me they often feel misunderstood and even resented by coworkers. When I ask them what would improve this situation, they say that management should educate the entire

---

10. "The Business Case for Child Care," Moms First, 2022, accessed January 2, 2024, momsfirst.us/childcare-report.

team on organizational policies such as leave or breastfeeding benefits, communicate flexible schedule arrangements, and model—and expect—a culture of support for working moms. Samantha, who works in an office environment, shared her story with me through social media:

> I got to my desk on my first day back, pulled up my calendar on the computer, and was shocked: my entire day had already been scheduled out by my colleagues, including a mandatory two-hour, all-staff meeting first thing in the morning. Followed by lunch with my boss to catch up on what I had missed over the course of a few months of leave. Followed by afternoon meetings back-to-back with other coworkers.
>
> My head was on overload. Where was the opportunity to get myself settled back in at a reasonable pace? Nobody asked how I was doing or how I saw the first days going to make the best of it. I was willing to hit the ground running, but I felt slammed immediately by everyone around me with no notice of the changes I'd just gone through. My boss definitely had not talked to my coworkers about a transition-back plan.
>
> I felt defeated and misunderstood. There was no communication or plan about my return to work, and I felt that from day one. I really felt pulled in all directions by my coworkers.

There are many reasons why working moms can feel unsupported by coworkers. Some moms I have talked with have said that older generations of parents resent how their own experience was met with more hardship: fewer legal protections, less workplace flexibility, or fewer benefits offered when they became a parent. In other instances, moms have reported to me that coworkers who are not parents may simply be unaware or unsupportive of unique issues like break-time laws for breastfeeding. Erika, the procurement officer I mentioned earlier, shared an experience that speaks to this point:

> An older female coworker said, "We can't be expected to provide those things, like a flexible work schedule, to you now. We didn't have that option when I was having children."
>
> Another colleague asked if I was planning on taking my full Family and Medical Leave Act (FMLA) time off when my baby was born. When I said that I was, she said, "I had thought you would come back sooner since the plant needs you." It's great that they appreciate my work role, but I feel like there should be understanding and acceptance for me to take my relatively minimal twelve weeks of time off in the scheme of the years I'm dedicating to the company. This same coworker followed up by saying to me, "Twenty-eight

years ago when I had a baby, I only had six weeks. You parents today are spoiled."

Emotionally, this hurts your feelings, because you hope that people will express joy and happiness for you becoming a mom and will want to see you succeed at work and home. It makes me feel sad that people at work aren't happy for me but are judgmental, with an attitude of "it must be nice" to have a reasonable benefit. I would have wanted these people to have had the same benefit back then, too, and I'm sorry they did not.

Also, these comments don't take into consideration how the job has changed. My job is all systems driven and can be done remotely, something that [has] advanced with technology in the decades since those parents had children and enables me to utilize flexible work options. I really do empathize with what they parented through, but times have changed, and I think our bosses need to reach out and do a better job creating a culture of acceptance of working mothers today.

Many parents, for many generations, have been forced by culture and company protocol to put job first and family second—or to hide the existence of family from the workplace. While moms tell me they feel a shift is happening among younger colleagues and bosses, where they are more welcoming of family into the workplace, there still appears to be generational conflict. Moms not only want strong communication between manager and working moms but also want managers to educate other stakeholders so that transition plans can unfold without obstacle, guilt, or resentment from the people working around and with them.

Benefits and Policies

In my job, I stay in a near-constant line of communication with all types of working moms. I prompt them regularly on social media to talk with me about work–life balance and the motherhood experience, and I also provide resources—advice from professionals, funding to organizations, and partnership with experts in the field of postpartum mental health and breastfeeding—to help them on this journey. As a result, my phone regularly blows up with messages from moms about work benefits that don't really benefit them. Moms are frustrated, as you can imagine, when well-intentioned benefits are better on paper than they are functional for the team the intend to serve. One mom shared with me:

> How would you feel in this situation? I was handed something from my boss called a "Remote Work Agreement." The form reads something like this: "Remote work is available to all company employees and can

be flexed as a partial schedule with a mix of in-person and remote work as well; options exist."

I selected the box [for] "3 days remote work, 2 days on-site" because the flexibility of being home some days would allow me an easier transition back after baby, reduce the hours my child is in daycare, give me a chance to get to doctor appointments, and more. I also felt I should be on-site sometimes to connect with supervisors and colleagues.

I ultimately received a rejection from my site supervisor. My job has no duties that require on-site presence; I just personally offered two days to stay physically engaged with the company. My boss was told by that supervisor that our site doesn't have to honor the flex work policy after all.

On paper, my company has a policy that seems like it supports work–life balance. But it doesn't exist. I feel really let down by my company.

Moms want you to *ask* them if the policies are working for them. Better yet, working moms want to be involved in the design of policies and benefits from the outset. How do moms think they could impact outcomes through these conversations? They have some really good ideas. For instance:

If I could have talked to the supervising manager about the remote-work request, I could have provided data to show that my personal metrics were not affected by this setup, but I was never given the chance to discuss.

During the two-month wait from when the application was submitted and the silence that followed, my boss advised me to set up a more permanent home office because she was sure that I would continue work from home. I did. I purchased a desk and a chair, second and third monitors, and all of the things I would need. This was money spent that was not going to be reimbursed, which I understood but was willing to do because of the schedule flexibility.

I am now out of that money—the desk sits empty, and the chair isn't in use. It's a space in my home being taken up as a constant reminder of the lack of communication and lack of support from my organization.

And Amanda, the nurse who couldn't easily reach the bottom-floor lactation room from the critical care unit on the top floor—who has since left the job—shared with me her attempts to try to improve her situation while she was still there:

I did eventually ask human resources why we couldn't have a lactation space closer to my unit on the top floor of the new hospital building. They said there was no space and what we [had was] "fine," and I just [needed] to plan for it.

There is no planning in critical care. Patient condition dictates when, where, and how long we can take a break.

When they built this hospital, very recently, they created a multimillion-dollar building of cutting-edge architecture and left the lactation room on the ground floor connected to the old building.

They had a chance to ask moms about the location of the lactation room and to literally build one into the design wherever it would work best for the people who need to use it. I wish they had asked for our input.

Bravo to your organization if you are checking all the boxes on legal requirements for lactation spaces and break times—even better if you have made these spaces comfortable and private—but regardless, ask the moms using this room if it is working out for them. Moms want policies and benefits to be designed with their voices included. Audit your existing programs and ask your working moms: *Is this program working in the way we intended?* You can do this through surveys (identified or anonymous), lunch gatherings, staff meetings, and even in exit interviews. Save the money on benefits or bells and whistles that don't really make a difference for the moms. The ideal benefits package for working moms is one that reflects what they want and need to be healthy and successful at your workplace: a win-win for you both.

The Bottom Line from New Moms

For ten years, I've heard the stories of thousands of new moms as they head back to work. And now I flag and forward their message to you: manager communication can either set the course for a successful transition back to work or spur an exit plan for the mom. I've outlined the major pain-point topics to give you a heads-up on the kinds of things moms would talk to you about if you asked. Here is a summary of the critical priorities where moms say they need you to ask about support—and then provide it:

- Mental health
- Flexible scheduling
- Childcare
- Support from coworkers
- Benefits and policies

When conversations about work/parenting challenges come out in the open, good results can happen—I'll tell you more about this in chapter six, when we'll hear again about Patricia, the mom who had the mental health breakdown in the office, and others who ultimately found success on the job after communication was strengthened with their managers. The critical thing to walk away with from this chapter is that every mom on your team needs to be asked what they specifically need from your organization. The personal reward and professional outcomes associated with a strong manager/working mom relationship are numerous—and later in the book, I'll give you some great real-life examples of how this plays out.

2

The Business Case for Supporting Working Moms

Maybe you have seen firsthand how working moms make for outstanding long-term employees and want to hire more to your team but aren't sure how to attract talent. Perhaps you are trying to meet a diversity, equity, and inclusion (DEI) goal because your organization finds itself losing talented women around the time they start a family. This chapter is going to help you make the business case for supporting working moms. It would be awesome if we could just examine the issue of supporting working moms from a feel-good point of view, but the truth is that many organizations and most of us managers must lead and make decisions based on profits and goals and with budgets always in mind. I'm going to equip you in this chapter with the data points and key arguments needed to bring everyone at your organization—even the most financially driven or resistant players—on board with supporting working moms.

Losing moms is unprofitable. Retaining and hiring moms to your teams and organization is additive. By examining the positive economic implications of supporting working moms, I can help equip you to convince less enthusiastic people in leadership and on your teams to implement supportive practices and policies. Even if higher leadership cannot be convinced, I can equip *you*, and as you'll hear time and time again throughout this book, managers can make a significant difference for the happiness and success of their employees, even on their own. You will learn in this chapter that the benefits of supporting working moms often exceed the costs of implementing the supports, particularly when you look at the cost of losing experienced and productive employees on your team. And being open and honest about cost and benefit of supporting working mothers also ultimately validates them as valuable members of the workforce: we give them power, status, visibility, and credit for making a tangible impact on our organization's bottom line. We help make them seen.

Retaining Moms Results in Short-Term Financial Savings

When supported by their managers and their organizations, working moms miss less work, stay healthier, improve your team morale, and—gasp—save *and* make your organization money! There are numerous data points to boost your argument to leadership and to your colleagues on why supporting working moms matters.

In a normal year—one that doesn't include a global pandemic and the Great Resignation—US businesses experience approximately $1 trillion (yes, trillion) in annual losses from employee turnover. And this figure accounts for only tangible expenses: "one-half to two times the employee's annual salary—and that's a conservative estimate."[1] This, of course, does not consider any other indirect or less trackable expenses, such as the impact on the longevity of *other* employees as people often stick together, the current market for recruitment of equally skilled replacement talent, the effect of the employee departure on contracts or grants or leadership roles, or the extra work effort put in by that employee. For instance, did the working mom you lost from your team spearhead volunteer initiatives in the company? Was this mom mentoring someone else on your team? Were they overseeing a program or project that was off job description? Did they help your company win an award for community or pro bono services? These

---

1. Shane McFeely and Ben Wigert, "This Fixable Problem Costs U.S. Businesses $1 Trillion," Gallup, March 13, 2019, www.gallup.com/workplace/247391/fixable-problem-costs-businesses-trillion.aspx.

are meaningful contributions to our organization's success that are hard to measure.

Turnover can sink profit and operational budget. However, turnover among moms is not and does not have to be inevitable. Managers, here is your call to action: support working moms so that they stay in their jobs. The organization's bottom line, and your team's success, depends on it.

Supporting Moms Results in Long-Term Financial Savings

Aside from the significant money saved immediately through retention, there are other unique and clever ways in which supporting working moms uniquely saves an organization money, increases productivity, and improves morale on your team. For example, numerous studies show that breastfed babies have fewer health issues than babies who are not breastfed.[2] What does this amount to for an employer? When their babies are healthier, the moms—and dads—in your workplace are more productive, missing fewer workdays and making fewer claims against

---

2. "The Business Case for Breastfeeding: For Business Managers," US Department of Health and Human Services, 2008, accessed January 2, 2024, www.womenshealth.gov/breastfeeding /breastfeeding-home-work-and-public/breastfeeding-and-going -back-work/business-case.

your insurance plans. Also, moms are more likely to come back to their previous job when their employer "provides a supportive environment for continued breastfeeding . . . [For example,] Mutual of Omaha's lactation support program led to a retention rate of 83 percent of their maternity workforce compared to the national average of only 59 percent. Another study of several companies with lactation programs showed a retention rate of 94.2 percent."[3]

Research has shown that breastfeeding can also improve a woman's long-term health, reducing diseases such as breast and ovarian cancer, high blood pressure, and diabetes, all of which could impact her stability on your team even after her children are grown.[4] The US Department of Health and Human Services has conducted research on the business case for breastfeeding supports in the workplace and offers strong evidence for managers to use in their organizations:[5]

---

3. "The Business Case for Breastfeeding," US Department of Health and Human Services.

4. "Breastfeeding Benefits Both Baby and Mom," Centers for Disease Control and Prevention, 2021, accessed January 2, 2024, www.cdc.gov/nccdphp/dnpao/features/breastfeeding-benefits/index.html.

5. "The Business Case for Breastfeeding," US Department of Health and Human Services.

- One major provider of health insurance saw significant benefit to offering robust lactation support—to the tune of "annual savings of $240,000 in health care expenses, 62 percent fewer prescriptions, and $60,000 savings in reduced absenteeism rates."

- Although 80 percent of its employees are male, the Los Angeles Department of Water and Power found that a lactation support program for mothers, fathers, and partners of male employees made a dramatic difference in reducing turnover and absenteeism rates for both male and female workers.

You can achieve these positive outcomes for your employees and their families—and savings for your organization—by offering time and space to use a breast pump and by talking with your moms to find out what else they need to reach their breastfeeding goals. Perhaps they need dedicated fridge space to store milk. For sure, moms want outlet access to connect their breast pumps, which might not be as available in an older building as you would think. Moms also say they ideally need a non-bathroom sink to wash their breast pump parts according to safety guidelines. You are sure to see the return on investment when you support workplace breastfeeding; the data is there to back you up.

And breastfeeding is just one example—you will find similar statistics for companies that support mental health.

For instance, on the issue of anxiety and insomnia, one study found that employers providing support services to address these issues had, overall, about a 20 percent reduction in health-care costs among employees who utilized the benefits compared to those who did not.[6] Organizations that do not provide support for mental health see higher costs, lower revenue and profits, and poor performance; conversely, organizations that support mental health for their teams see greater positive outcomes. As with all benefits offered, this support also makes your organization competitive. In fact, one study showed that upward of 60 percent of employees will only take a job offer that supports mental health and other similar wellness benefits.[7] Managers and organizations who promote the mental, physical, and emotional well-being of their employees will reap the rewards of healthier, happier, and more productive team members in the long term. They will also position their organizations to be competitive in the job marketplace.

---

6. Michael Darden, "Fortune 50 Retailer Saves 19.6% in Health Care Costs by Addressing Employee Mental Health," Big Health, January 31, 2022, www.bighealth.com/blog/fortune-50-retailer-saves-costs-by-addressing-mental-health/.

7. "Effects of Mental Health in the Workplace and Why It's Important," Paychex, April 4, 2023, www.paychex.com/articles/human-resources/workplace-mental-health-effects.

Working Moms Bring Valuable Skills to Your Teams

Working moms tend to be exceptionally "Gumby-like" in their ability to pivot, manage crises well, and improve team morale. In *On the Brink: A Fresh Lens to Take Your Business to New Heights*, corporate anthropologist Andi Simon writes that "the future of your business needs people who can adapt, show flexibility, and enable an organization to change to meet the new demands of customers and the technology that is coming now. Women have been able to discard the 'way we always have done it' mindset and learn new ways to do the tasks of daily living in the office and out."[8] In my experience as a business leader, I have found working moms to be excellent at identifying problems quickly and offering a series of realistic solutions. Juggling breastfeeding, limited sleep, pediatrician visits and their own medical appointments, financial planning, maintaining a family calendar, cooking meals, cleaning, listening, and attending to the needs of small human beings, even with robust partner support, you learn fast as a mom how to fit more into a day than ever before.

---

8. Andi Simon, *On the Brink: A Fresh Lens to Take Your Business to New Heights* (Austin, TX: Greenleaf Book Group Press, 2016).

When I asked my network what they think about this issue—the valuable and unique traits they bring as moms to their jobs—they said:

"I get jobs done more efficiently now than before baby because I have family demands and time at home, and I have proposed new ways of doing the same tasks more efficiently since I have less time to work with and motivation to get things done."

"I'm the person on our team who defuses emotionally heated conversations now, which is an important role on the team. Becoming a mom, I had to develop my own self-regulation skills and [help] my kids do so, too; I use those skills to help in meetings where the conversations are charged up, and I think I help keep the peace a lot."

"I feel like I have developed a super-efficiency power at home that I now bring to work, and my manager has noticed and given me more projects to lead as a result."

"I'm more understanding and empathetic in patient care now because I have experienced a different perspective on life changes."

"Because you have to hold your baby while listening to a conference call, while making dinner, with a load of laundry in the wash, you learn how to juggle a lot without being asked to do it, how to be the initiator."

Strong work ethic, growth-mindset personality traits, and the ability to juggle tasks to the extreme are not consistent across all mom employees, but most people recognize that motherhood demands the development of new life skills that not only support parenting but can translate into the workplace. In fact, studies show that most Americans agree that "moms excel in organizational leadership, are better listeners, calmer in a crisis, more diplomatic, and better team players."[9]

Other managers I've interacted with over the last decade tell me that working moms on their teams sometimes apply themselves more so than their peers at work, in part to overcome the perception that the demands of motherhood interfere with work; these moms tend to be goal-oriented employees who want to prove themselves to managers while getting the work done efficiently to get home and have a rewarding personal life.

Increased financial pressure also motivates working moms—and other parents, too, of course. The demands of children to feed, childcare to pay for, and college to save for drives moms to achieve work stability and success. Any prior notion that moms work just to supplement dad's income in a secondary position is outdated: "In about

---

9. "Modern Family Index 2018," Bright Horizons, 2018, accessed January 2, 2024, www.brighthorizons.com/newsroom/modern -family-index-2018.

50 percent of American families, women [have become] the sole or co-breadwinners in their households."[10] What does this mean for you? Working moms are high-capacity, regulated, driven team members who are problem-solving big issues, applying diplomatic skills in meetings, and getting work done efficiently with limited time and resources. This is who we want on our teams!

Supporting Moms Creates Future Women Leaders

Supporting working moms creates the next generation of women leaders in organizations. How so? Managers directly influence the future of women in leadership by creating a workplace where younger, newer employees who become parents stay in the workforce, excel in their jobs, train and build on their skills, and aspire to move upward. Why does that matter? Because organizations that employ more women leaders—from manager all the way up to CEO—are more profitable; as a CNBC report explains, "Innovation is fundamentally the result of trial and error. And if you're able to bring different skills to the process . . .

10. Khadijah Plummer, "Women in the Workplace: Statistics and Trends," Contact Monkey, updated June 21, 2023, www.contact monkey.com/blog/women-in-workplace.

you do a better job."[11] Diversity in this way is a key indicator to team and organization success.

Unfortunately, women still do not easily nor magically appear in higher levels of leadership; they must be advanced in the employment pipeline for years—including retaining and supporting them through early motherhood. If you have a rotating group of younger women on your teams who are leaving for competing organizations with better support, you are not as likely to have a pool of qualified women to rise in the ranks. As a manager, you may feel more focused on moving members of your team along the path of advancement within a department or through entry to midlevel jobs and not be as centered on higher leadership roles. However, you can play an instrumental role in cultivating the next generation of women leaders. We only advance women to the upper echelon of organizational leadership by creating mom-supportive workplaces where they stay and advance while achieving their family goals.

11. Yoni Blumberg, "Companies with More Female Executives Make More Money—Here's Why," CNBC, March 2, 2018, www.cnbc.com /2018/03/02/why-companies-with-female-managers-make-more -money.html.

Working Mothers Are the Current and Future Talent

Statistics show that moms in the workforce over the age of twenty-five have higher levels of education than the rest of your workforce of the same age bracket—and "the millennial generation is the first generation in history in which women are more educated than men."[12] Meaning if your hiring objective is to pull from the most educated candidates—or if the jobs you must fill require a certain degree or higher level of education—you will be drawing from a candidate pool of working mothers or from women who are highly likely to become moms in the future.

This also serves as a good reminder on the retention front as well: if we lose a working-mom employee, we are likely to hire another or future working mother to that role. It is becoming increasingly impossible to avoid hiring working moms, which I hope is not the case where you work, but regardless, the point needs to be made. Are you ready with

---

12. Cheridan Christnacht and Briana Sullivan, "About Two-Thirds of the 23.5 Million Working Women with Children Under 18 Worked Full-Time in 2018," United States Census Bureau, May 8, 2020, www.census.gov/library/stories/2020/05/the-choices-working -mothers-make.html; Jillian Berman, "Millennial Women Are More Educated Than Men But Are Still Paid Less," Institute for Women's Policy Research, accessed January 2, 2024, statusofwomen data.org/coverage/millennial-women-are-more-educated-than -men-but-are-still-paid-less/.

the policies, benefits, and culture to support the next generation of working moms who will staff your teams?

Working Moms Are Consumers

When I worked in my first nonprofit organization, which provided educational resources and conferences for women elected to state governments, I was surprised how few of the legislators were moms of younger kids. Most women in these roles had older children or no children at all. Over the years in talking to these leaders, I learned that the environment in most elected positions is not the least bit supportive of working moms. Many of the women agreed this was a problem—particularly because on issues of education, health care, and topics that so directly impacted younger women, they would have liked to have seen that demographic in the elected ranks. However, not only do these women have to take on exposing their personal lives publicly to the media and constituents, but also, the hours are demanding and the culture is not one that traditionally welcomes kids into the fold. It was startling to me that a huge demographic of voters—working moms of younger children—did not have direct demographic representation in elected office, and I hope the situation will change. I believe there is a valuable lesson here for managers: hire, retain, and support working mothers in your organization because there is value in having people on the inside of the organization who are representative of the people you serve.

In fact, in the United States, 83 percent of household buyers are moms.[13] And as is so aptly pointed out in consumer studies, these moms make decisions for everyone. We aren't just talking baby items—we're talking food, other consumables, clothing, large household purchases, and so forth. If you are in any type of industry where a consumer drives your bottom line—service, product and brand, health care, technology, media, safety, insurance—you are working to appeal to a mom decision-maker. Whether the roles you manage on your team are in administration, labor, data, marketing, customer service, or something else, having insight and trust with the mom demographic from the inside of your team can help you provide better products and services. Clearly, as the owner and founder of a breast-feeding products company, I tap into the working moms on my team every single day for their insights and experience. But I was aware of doing this even when I worked in a non-profit that advocated for often elderly consumers needing

---

13. Erin Fabio, "Marketing to Moms as a Consumer Group," Forbes .com, March 8, 2023, www.forbes.com/sites/forbesagencycouncil /2023/03/08/marketing-to-moms-as-a-consumer-group/?sh =59c10faa4d78.

home care and nursing home care. At that organization, the working moms knew a lot about caregiving, budgeting, and future planning, which was so relevant to the topics we advocated for and resources we created in long-term care. Think about your industry and whether working moms on your team are additive in helping you to understand your customer base.

Six Ways Supporting Working Moms Pays Off

In the sections above, I have outlined six possible ways supporting working moms is financially good for your organization:

1. Retaining moms results in short-term financial savings
2. Supporting moms results in long-term financial savings
3. Working moms bring valuable skills to your teams
4. Supporting moms creates future women leaders
5. Working moms are the current and future talent
6. Working moms are consumers

Equipped with excellent reasons—maybe even a wake-up call that supporting working moms is an inevitable requirement of any successful organization—I want to offer you further insight from my experience of observing and connecting with working moms in my network in ways you may have not previously considered.

Women Are Watching

Working mothers with whom I meet frequently say that they are *planners*. I recognize that moms are not a monolith, which is really the premise of this book—each mom has unique needs that managers need to learn about—and not all moms have a plan for work and children. It is a privilege to work in a job where you have *any* choice in the planning of your next career move. With that said, research studies show that there is a concerted effort on the part of many working moms to craft a "strategic career design" far before they become parents to ensure their success in both work and motherhood.[14] And this is precisely what moms in my network have to say. Why does this matter to you as a manager? It matters because women are assessing your organizational policies and your management culture of support for working moms before they become mothers. They are

---

14. Matthias Krapf, Heinrich W. Ursprung, and Christian Zimmermann, "Parenthood and Productivity of Highly Skilled Labor: Evidence from the Groves of Academe," Federal Reserve Bank of St. Louis, 2014, https://doi.org/10.20955/wp.2014.001.

making observations about working-mom conditions for *years* prior to starting a family.

Not offering support has retention repercussions far before a mom makes the transition out of and back to work. In fact, working moms' decisions about longevity on your team may stem much further back than you realize. Taylor, a mom working in distribution and fulfillment, shared her story with me through Instagram on this very point:

> *When I started out in my career, I was driven; I wanted to be the best because I'm competitive in my job but also knew early on that I wanted to be able to financially support a family someday. I worked very hard at the first company right out of college, doubling what I was making in the first three years, and I thought, Okay, six figures. Now we can have a family. But then, after seeing the challenges that a close friend in our company who had a little boy faced, my eyes were opened: the kind of workplace I needed wasn't just high pay—it was flexibility and support, too.*
>
> *I made a career move away from that financially secure job that didn't have other support so that I could start a family and have strong mental health. The company I moved to cared deeply about balancing [work and life], would let you try a lot of new things, and even offered mentorship. I spent two years evaluating whether this company met my needs for*

flexibility and outward support of employees who had kids, and when I felt that it did, I had a baby.

Taylor's story is like that of many moms I have encountered, such as Mackenzie, who serves as corporate counsel for a midsize health-care system and shared the following with me:

About three years before we wanted to start a family, I looked to transition in my career from a very unsupportive working environment to one that had benefits, a supportive manager and team, and that offered some level of paid leave. I didn't need those supports right away, but I was thinking ahead to starting a family and wanted to establish somewhere ahead of time that offered me what I needed for a family.

The message to managers is clear: if we do not create a culture of support for working moms on our teams—or send clear signals to our employees that we would do so if we ever had a working mom on our team—many of the moms we hire will eventually leave. As managers, we cannot "beat the clock" with women by hiring, promoting, and advancing them before they are pregnant and expecting them to stay in an unsupportive workplace. In fact, I have learned from the experiences of these moms that they often take the job at an unsupportive company—knowingly or unknowingly—complete training and gain experience, and then move to your industry competitors who are offering more working-mom support. You will also find that your competitors are using this support as a recruitment tool to poach your best team members.

Support Is a Recruitment Tool

Supporting working mothers is a key factor not only in retention but in *recruitment*, too. In numerous studies, women say that they scope out your organization for supports before they apply or take a job offer. It is becoming easier and easier to learn about company culture ahead of the hiring process since ratings, reviews, and more are readily available on the internet.

In one survey, 69 percent of moms said that childcare benefits were a top priority in their job search.[15] My conversation with new mom Gabrielle confirmed that moms are poised and ready to ask you about support before they set foot on your teams:

> *During my job search, I asked at the end of all my interviews, "Can you tell me what kind of accommodations you give to breastfeeding moms?" I put it back on the employer to explain to me how they are*

15. "The Business Case for Child Care," Moms First, 2022, accessed January 2, 2024, momsfirst.us/childcare-report/.

supporting their working moms, which was very tell-ing about how they comply with laws and whether they go the extra mile to support moms. I got a couple of offers and chose the one that had a wellness room and knew a lot about the support they offer to parents during the interview process.

As a manager, are you ready to answer questions from potential new hires about working-mom support? Are you able to give more than a scripted line about benefits from the personnel policy or employee handbook and instead offer a comprehensive, thoughtful answer that is going to attract the most educated, top-value, diverse candidates? If not, this is the time to get started. In chapter six, I'll give you a step-by-step road map for conversations with your currently employed moms that you can use as a basis to strengthen your supportive policies and culture. In this road map, I will also cover being fully prepared to address working-mom support during the interview process.

The Laws Say You Must Support Working Moms

My book is focused on creating the will for managers to support working moms by equipping them with all the reasons this makes good sense for teams and organizations. However, it is also important to note that federal laws also require several supports for working moms, which I will outline below. Because your state may have additional laws on the books, it is also important to talk to your human resources department or do your own research with reputable working-family organizations and government agencies to learn what might apply in your location.

Like the enforcement of civil rights, these federal laws are especially important for the most vulnerable parents who have no other protections from being retaliated against or being taken advantage of for their familial status or needs at their workplace. Specifically, since I started writing this book, the US Congress passed the Providing Urgent Maternal Protections (PUMP) for Nursing Mothers Act (S. 1658/H.R. 3110) as part of the omnibus spending package of 2022. This federal legislation requires employers with over fifty employees, and those with under fifty employees if not a hardship on the organization, to provide time and space for breastfeeding parents to pump during the workday. With the passage of this legislation, an additional nine million parents were covered with lactation support in the workplace. The Pregnant Workers Fairness Act, which requires employers to offer reasonable accommodations for medical issues related to pregnancy and childbirth, was also passed as part of that same omnibus package and is poised to provide significant and extended support on a range of pregnancy and postpartum topics relevant to working moms, including time off for mental health services, additional breastfeeding support, physical accommodations during pregnancy and after childbirth, and more.

The Feds are slowly but surely taking note: supporting working mothers makes strong economic sense. For example, a study used by advocates of the PUMP Act legislation found that if 90 percent of mothers in the United States breastfed for six months, there would be savings of $13 billion in medical costs.[16] There is still a long way to go until the laws afford moms the support they need to effectively navigate working and parenthood—paid leave, equal and better pay, affordable and available childcare, maternal health care, resources to address disparities in support and care. However, the minimum of support as protected by law is indeed going *up*. Where once providing a place to use a breast pump made a workplace competitively supportive, that support is now mandated in virtually all workplaces. If you want to be more than "just compliant," be competitive in the marketplace, and attract the best working mom talent, you will need to offer more than the minimum.

The starting point to being competitive in your support to working moms is to ask moms on your teams: *How can we build on the support we are providing now?*

---

16. Melissa Bartick, "The Burden of Suboptimal Breastfeeding in the United States: A Pediatric Cost Analysis," American Academy of Pediatrics, May 1, 2010, publications.aap.org/pediatrics /article-abstract/125/5/e1048/72534/The-Burden-of-Suboptimal -Breastfeeding-in-the.

What else can we do to support you? The moms I interact with who are *not* happy at work often already have the bare minimum provided, but it is not adequate to meet their support needs. I think back to the example I shared in the introduction of Amanda, the nurse who had the legally required time and space for pumping but did not have enough time to pump because the space provided was compliant but not geographically desirable for her job in demanding ICU care. Imagine what Amanda and her manager could have accomplished in a series of simple conversations about support.

Successful DEI Programs Support Moms—Not Just Hire Women

I have shared reasons why supporting working moms will save you money in retention while growing your organization through the unique talents and perspectives and educational qualifications working moms do and will bring to your teams. Often, another reason women are brought on to teams is to support diversity, equity, and inclusion (DEI) goals. To win federal contracts, to gain clients, to enhance reputation and credibility among consumers and investors, and to be eligible for nonprofit grants, your teams will need to demonstrate diversity—even at the highest levels of corporate America, such as at Goldman Sachs, where the CEO, David Solomon, said that they won't take public any company that doesn't have a woman on the board.[17] The tide is shifting on society's perspective of women in leadership, and successful organizations will hire and retain women at all levels. However, many organizations approach gender diversity from a butt-in-seat approach—that is, hire enough women to balance out the men or reach some kind of percentage or number goal. These same organizations are shocked when their thoughtfully acquired new hires later exit for more supportive workplaces. A new mom shared with me how her law firm has a significant decline in women lawyers by the time they reach the senior levels. At hiring, there is a meaningful number of women in the junior ranks, but the long hours, lack of flexibility, pervasive "mommy track," and overall lack of a supportive culture in her firm has these women exiting before they hit the leadership levels for other firms or legal jobs that promote opportunities for support.

Law firms are likely not the only organizations hiring women and losing working moms. A recent study found that "more than two-thirds of women under 30 say they care more than they did two years ago about flexibility and company commitment to well-being" and that "manager

---

17. Kim Elsesser, "Goldman Sachs Won't Take Companies Public If They Have All-Male Corporate Boards," Forbes.com, January 23, 2020, www.forbes.com/sites/kimelsesser/2020/01/23 /goldman-sachs-wont-take-companies-public-if-they-have-all -male-corporate-boards/?sh=777a68a09475.

support is deeply important to all employees, and it's one of the top three factors women consider when deciding whether to join or stay with a company."[18] Women who become moms don't stay at organizations because of the presence of other women there; they stay because there are supportive managers to help them meet their goals in career and motherhood.

A recent study of the highest-performing organizations with DEI programs found that these companies provided additional benefits to employees beyond just hiring women and minorities, including ongoing support for mental health, time off for miscarriage, childcare services, parental leave with a commitment of returning to the same role, career development programs, and the requirement for managers to have conversations with employees about what they need to be successful. These top-performing companies were also transparent about what employees were asking managers for in the way of support and gave training to managers to implement everything in this list.[19] DEI success will not arrive through hiring alone; by solely

18. "Women in the Workplace Study: The State of Women in Corporate America," LeanIn.org, 2022, accessed January 2, 2024, leanin.org/women-in-the-workplace.

19. Emily Field, Alexis Krivkovich, Sandra Kügele, et al., "Women in the Workplace 2023," McKinsey and Company, October 5, 2023, www.mckinsey.com/featured-insights/diversity-and-inclusion/women-in-the-workplace.

focusing on the hiring process, you'll burn through talent and find yourself behind the curve compared to others in your industry or sector.

When I was speaking with Taylor, the mom in operations and human resources within the distribution-and-fulfillment industry whom I mentioned earlier in this chapter, she shared: "One time I was sitting in a diversity-and-retention meeting, and our executive vice president told me that we could solve our diversity retention gap by 'promoting women before they had a chance to get pregnant so they'd stay.'" Of course, this is an utterly backward—and offensive—way of thinking to increase the number of women in organizations. It is never going to work because, as Taylor demonstrated when she left that six-figure leadership job for a better work culture, moms will still leave if they aren't supported. They exit after you have trained them, invested resources into their career development, instituted them as mentors to other employees, or maybe even put them in charge of the DEI work, which women are often asked to spearhead. Taylor concluded: "In order to stay in a company, women need to see other women being truly supported, and the conversation of how that support will happen and how valued they are needs to be taking place well before they decide to start a family."

Working mothers are strong candidates to help diversify your organization not only through gender. Moms as a demographic are racially, ethnically, and culturally diverse and bring varied life experiences and perspectives that I spoke of earlier.[20] Hiring women and working moms will achieve many of your diversity goals; however, managers, leaders, and teams must look at *supporting* working moms as another critical part of their diversity programs. The will and resources to support working moms absolutely requires leadership buy-in, but as I have discussed here, the "doing" happens on the ground at the manager level. I hope your leadership has a strong interest in diversity goals, and now you can convey what the data supports: a successful DEI program requires working-mother support in place before the hires even begin.

The Mommy Track Is Code for an Unsupportive Workplace

If you find that many of the women in your organization and on your teams are opting for or being forced into the so-called mommy track—forgoing promotions or advancement to roles like manager, director, and partner; dropping out of full-time to permanent part-time employment; or not taking on new projects—it is time to evaluate whether your supports for working moms are adequate. If you can

20. "The Working Moms Report," Breezy and Après Group, December 2, 2021, accessed January 2, 2024, breezy.hr/blog/working-moms-report.

picture what the mommy track looks like in your company, name the people on it, and see how it manifests in your organization (e.g., the team considers remote workers less than those who come into the office, or that woman that you were certain was going to be partner has taken a sudden step back), your organization may not be doing enough to support moms. Working moms are Fortune 500 CEOs. Working moms are excelling at any job out there. Of course, I wish for every employee to have self-determination and choices such as to be a stay-at-home mother, to have a change of heart and make a career move, or to work fewer hours. But a "track" is a different concept than the individual choices made by employees. The mommy track is code for an unsupportive workplace.

As managers, we need to remember that flexibility and supports do not equal "less committed" or "less capable" or "less performing"—in fact, flexibility can be a gateway to bigger success for our teams. Throughout this chapter, I have demonstrated to you that working moms add value to your bottom line; that they are already the most highly educated labor pool to draw from; that they solve labor shortages, spur innovation, and outperform their peers in leadership roles. If the COVID-19 pandemic demonstrated anything to us about the changing workplace, it showed us that it is possible to make a big life pivot, excel in our redefined job roles, and drive success at organizations while we go remote or work under intense pressures. This is the work landscape for moms on an everyday basis, with or without a pandemic. They can succeed while working flexibly, while juggling a lot of responsibilities, while working under immense pressure—the evidence says they thrive in this intensity when they have the resources and support they need.

Working moms are not on a mommy track unless you place them there, to the detriment of your organization. We want to hire these problem-solvers, the do-it-all-ers, and we must support them so they can stay the course with us.

3

Why Managers Are Not Talking to Moms About Support

There must be a reason why managers aren't talking to working moms about their support needs. Most of the moms I talked with had *never* had a conversation about support outside of receiving information about personnel policies. It may or may not surprise you to learn that most managers are *afraid* to talk with their employees; in fact, a recent poll found that 69 percent of managers say communication is a struggle with their teams.[1] Identifying

---

1. Steve Farber, "A Recent Study Showed That 70 Percent of Leaders Are Scared to Talk with Their Employees. Here's a Solution,"

the barriers for managers to initiate conversations with working moms about support is a key part of overcoming this reluctance.

This chapter will examine and acknowledge the real and impactful cultural, economic, and legal issues that can block manager communication with working moms. The goal of this analysis is to help you as a manager grow in your awareness of any bias or anxiety that might be hindering you from taking the necessary steps to support moms. By understanding these barriers, dispelling myths, and sorting through feelings that may be associated with parenthood-related topics, this chapter will help clear the way for you to initiate these important conversations, which I've laid out in a road map for you in chapter six.

Lack of Firsthand Experience

It is human nature to feel uncomfortable confronting topics we do not have firsthand experience with ourselves. This can be a barrier to tackling a topic that you feel unequipped to address. I get it. I recently took the Girl Scout troop of one of my daughters to the Smithsonian bug exhibit, and even in that low-risk situation with second graders who will

---

Inc., March 7, 2018, www.inc.com/steve-farber/study-shows-69 -percent-of-leaders-are-scared-to-talk-with-their-employees-heres -a-solution.html.

believe just about anything you say, I spent a fair amount of time educating myself on arthropods before leading them through the exhibit. To my surprise, several members of the public joined in for my "lecture," so I'm grateful I researched the subject before I sounded ridiculous in front of a group of strangers! If you're like me, you probably landed in this leadership role as manager, boss, or supervisor because you excel at preparing information. Other than the bug lecture, I've also found myself in a large conference room speaking on a highly controversial public policy topic with national media present. You bet I prepared a lot for that one. One of the key aspects in all my communication prep, whether a Google search about bugs or extensive media training for what became my speech quoted in *Time* magazine the next day, is finding a way to connect personally to the topic at hand. I do that in every event, team briefing, and Girl Scout meeting I lead.

If you were making a pitch or presenting results of Q4 performance to your leadership, you would take the time to pull together talking points and data, read the latest news or literature on your topic, or perhaps even interview individuals or attend a training first yourself. In the same vein, nobody expects a manager without personal experience as a new parent to relate or know the "right" thing to say off the bat. But you *can* prepare for this without becoming a mom! Let's start here and learn together, and by the end of this book, you'll be so well informed and prepared that you'll even be able to help other managers support working moms. You may not be an expert mom yourself, but you will become an expert communicator with moms.

Building connections with employees—in this case, new moms—never requires a shared experience but does require your engagement as manager. You've already taken a big step to understand the working-mom experience by reading this book and learning through the stories told and data presented. Within your own organization, you can do more specific research. Observe and listen to your team and your colleagues. What kinds of challenges or topics are you hearing parents in your organization talk about? These challenges and topics do not have to come from someone you manage; they could be expressed by someone more senior than you or in a different department. Just listen to the conversations in the office about parenting. View this like your Google search.

Inside my own team, I observe frequent stress regarding childhood illnesses. Kids get sick a lot, and that presents a tremendous amount of pressure on working parents. I learn by listening to the watercooler chatter—as a remote team at my business, we have a Slack channel for this kind of personal talk, and while I try to let the team have some space from me, the boss, I pop in from time to time keep tabs on what is going on culturally in the organization. What is it that parents are saying about work/life challenges? My team tells me that flexibility with schedules and remote work are hugely helpful ways to reduce this stress, particularly in the winter when viral illnesses run rampant. Tuning in and listening to the team's conversations about parenting, and engaging by asking questions or expressing empathy, may help you feel more in-the-know about the hot-button topics facing the moms on your team. Sometimes, when someone is on their fourth family virus in eight weeks, I send a gift card for dinner delivery. And it comes back to you tenfold; just the other day, my customer service representative sent *me* a gift card for coffee to perk me up! I was amazed by the generosity and thoughtfulness returned and love working in a culture like this myself. Tapping in and listening allows me to be an engaged and informed manager who can show support through my actions.

Even if it's not the norm—or perhaps just impossible because of the large size—in your organization for bosses to participate in casual conversation with employees, there are creative ways you can find out what people are talking about. For instance, the moms I polled from larger organizations with a more formal approach to feedback preferred systems where employees receive and give feedback to senior management, often in a "360-degree" style, where multiple people weigh in on how management is performing. These working moms also preferred anonymous surveys so that they can feel comfortable giving complete input without real or perceived fear of retaliation. Another working mom I spoke with in a company of five thousand employees said that their CEO allows any member of the team to email them directly with feedback, creating a sense of transparency and responsiveness about work culture.

Once you start listening and observing, you might discover that your team is totally silent about their new parenting woes. I will dig into this subject in depth in chapter four, but for now, let me assure you that silence does not mean these issues do not exist. If you have new parents on your teams and there is no parenting chatter, you are probably operating in a hindered communication environment for those employees. I have yet to come across a new mom who has zero concerns about work–life balance or told me, "Nope, I don't need any support!"

If no one is talking—and I hope you desire to change that—you may need to go outside of your organization to warm up your knowledge on these issues. One great starting point is to talk to parents in your life outside of work. Ask your friends, a sibling, your own parents, a neighbor, the friend at the gym who just had a kid—what has it been like going back to work as a new mom? What are the stresses, the challenges? What do they wish they had in place to make work more successful? Probe! In my experience, test driving an awkward conversation with someone in a lower-stakes situation can really take the edge off as a manager when approaching employees. I remember a great conversation with someone we hired for web development in a previous nonprofit job, who came to me and asked, "I have a colleague that just had a baby, and I wanted to show my support for her breastfeeding, but it's awkward. How do I talk about that?" How awesome that this guy did a trial run of this conversation with me! I was able to give him a few gift ideas for the new mom and helped him practice a line or two that wouldn't put him in an awkward spot.

During the time of writing this book, I had a team member with a first baby in the neonatal intensive care unit (NICU). I stayed in touch with her via text message around the time of her delivery. While I am a mother, I have never had a baby in the NICU; it is truly a different experience than the ones I had with my girls, who were born on or after their due dates and came home straight away and in full health. I followed my team member's lead on their comfort level of conversation, but I asked a lot of questions since this was a topic I did not know as much about. I also reached out to a friend who had a baby in a NICU for some advice on how to talk about these issues, and I even did—you guessed it—a Google search for "best ways to support a parent with a NICU baby." These are the kinds of manager questions I developed as I researched how to connect with this mom:

1. Would you like to hear from us while you are out on leave or be disconnected from me/the team? How would you like to communicate?

2. We know this isn't what you expected from your birth experience; what can we do to support you?
3. How is your mental health?
4. Are there any other parents in the NICU who are in the same position as you and can offer support? Who is there on-site to support you?

You do not have to have breastfed or given birth or had a baby in the NICU or even parented to be empathetic to new parents. And if these topics do make you feel uncomfortable, awkward, or anxious, that's okay; they are a bit anxiety provoking for moms, too! I'll share a few ideas in chapter six for how you might break the ice and prepare yourself to have the important managerial conversations with new moms that they deserve and that you and your organization will benefit from. Do not let lack of personal experience stand in the way of connecting with your team.

Anxiety about Liability, Laws, and Lawsuits

You might have a reasonable understanding of the Family and Medical Leave Act (FMLA) and how this does or does not relate to your organization's policies for family leave. But do you know the ins and outs of the Pregnancy Discrimination Act? How about the ways in which the Americans with Disabilities Act prohibits discrimination based on pregnancy-related disabilities, separate from other policies mentioned here?[2] What does your state say about pregnancy, caregiving, adoption, fertility treatment, bereavement, disability, and breastfeeding? If you work in a larger organization, you likely have a human resources department that tracks policies and trains managers, but I would guess a fair number of managers either do not remember all the details from those training sessions or may work within organizations that are a lot smaller. Smaller organizations may not have routine training on these policies, or, because of being pressured for time and resources, they may have a lag in learning about changes to the laws.

I've worked in a number of organizations where keeping on top of the rules was tremendously difficult—often, we learned about them on an as-needed basis. *Okay, we have a person who is pregnant on the staff—what are the rules about this? Quick, we need to develop a maternity leave policy!* Being overwhelmed or even scared of the rules is frequently at the top of the list of reasons managers tell me they are scared to talk to moms. I feel that, too. However, you are more likely as a manager or organization to risk legal action with a parent when there is an environment of noncommunication, bias, and fear. Resentment builds.

---

2. "Fact Sheet for Small Businesses: Pregnancy Discrimination," US Equal Employment Opportunity Commission, accessed January 2, 2024, www.eeoc.gov/laws/guidance/fact-sheet-small-businesses -pregnancy-discrimination.

Miscommunications happen. Tensions escalate. Action occurs. I encourage you to not let the mountain of rules stop you from making human connections that will spur better communication and lessen the chance of a hostile environment or misunderstanding.

There is no law that prohibits you from being a good listener or empathetic leader. In chapter five, I will share ways in which communication is a proven tool for manager–employee success, if not the most important way to get top performance from employees and curb any escalated situations. It is also important to remember that all these rules are often just the baseline of protection for workers: you can and should exceed what they offer in terms of support, benefits, and respect, in every way. I have said it before, and I think it merits saying it again: in this competitive job climate, it is not enough to do the minimum required for employees by law.

One manager I spoke with while writing this book said, "There is a fear that if we talk to workers about their full set of rights or benefits, they will want to use them." Keeping people in the dark because of your own biases about what benefits they should or should not have, or out of an economic concern for the organization, is never going to amount to team success. You will lose employees who will go on to work for compliant organizations that are transparent about their policies and support—many moms I have spoken to have left their jobs for this exact reason.

You could earn a reputation as an unsupportive or hostile place to work. It is possible some workers do not know the scope of their rights, but as a manager, I would not be able to sleep at night knowing that keeping information from people is how I led my team. And if your leadership wants to run the organization this way, consider leaving before you get into trouble.

I believe the biggest legal and retention risks come through bias, assumptions, keeping employees in the dark, and either a lack of manager knowledge of the rules or simply not prioritizing implementation of required supports because of your workload. Looking through the legal literature, it is remarkable how the advice for managers of a decade ago is still relevant today: "Managers are entitled to their views about how families should raise their children, but these opinions have no place in the office and, in fact, can give rise to significant legal liability if they're expressed there. There's a very easy way to find out whether a new mother wants a promotion that will require longer hours: *Ask*."[3] The risk is not in asking about support; *it is in not asking.*

---

3. Joan C. Williams and Amy J. C. Cuddy, "Will Working Mothers Take Your Company to Court?" *Harvard Business Review*, September 2012, hbr.org/2012/09/will-working-mothers-take-your -company-to-court.

Worries About Not Being Able to Say Yes

What if I ask a mom what they need and they request a schedule we cannot accommodate or submit a purchase order for breastfeeding supplies that we do not have the budget for? These are real questions, real fears, submitted to me by managers in my business network. A few years back, I was asked by a local government–funded organization to come to their building and help set up a lactation space for breastfeeding employees. This happened before it was required by law to have one of these spaces, and they were trying to do the right thing by their moms. While they took the initiative in asking for my help in picking the right furniture and amenities and such, I could tell they were terrified of overpromising and underdelivering, hence why they nervously asked for my outsider mom perspective. (But I love that they asked for help; they enlisted me, a working mom, to give them some firsthand experience in crafting good support—bravo!)

The fear of not being able to "meet the request" is a frequent response when I poll managers about barriers to initiating conversations with new moms. You may well understand that you must meet any legal obligations regardless of how you feel about parents or the laws, but it might be scary when the moms on your team ask for those above-and-beyond or gray-area benefits. How do you handle this and not let it hinder you from having these important conversations with your working moms to begin with?

First, it's about compromise. I was just talking to a friend who supervises a large office in a low-budget clinical setting. She had a breastfeeding mother on her team put in a request for her own refrigerator to store milk, a dorm-sized fridge in the $150-plus range and outside their restricted budget. My friend asked me, "Do I have to provide the fridge by law?" The answer was no—the federal law and the laws in her state said she must provide time and space for breastfeeding, but not a fridge. But I asked my friend whether she could compromise in a way that showed an effort to meet the needs of the employee without breaking her budget. Based on my own experience, this employee had a legitimate need. It is difficult to store breast milk sanitarily in a huge office setting with ice packs all day or in a jam-packed communal fridge, where you run the risk of someone throwing out or contaminating your hard-earned milk.

My friend came up with the idea to purchase a smaller soda-pop fridge, the eight-can type, for under fifty dollars, which this employee could use in her own office, with the assumption that the company could later keep the fridge in inventory for future employees with the same need. Is this the ideal solution that the employee wanted or needed? Probably not. But can this employee find adequate support with the small temporary fridge as backup storage of their milk? Yes. And I believe your employee will feel supported, even if the solution was more modest than requested. So, consider how you could ask and meet your moms' needs, even if it requires a compromise.

And you don't always have to compromise. It *is* okay to say no. You can turn down an employee's request so long as it is not legally required; your job as manager is to work within the parameters of the organization's policies, budget, and realistic operations of your team. When I polled the moms in my network, more than 50 percent said they would prefer a manager ask them what they need for support even if the answer ends up being a no. The process of asking and explaining the no makes them feel heard. To be clear, the moms tell me that "fake caring"—that is, asking what they need knowing you are going to say no to everything no matter what—is not the same as an authentic ask. Moms can read your intentions and body language on this loud and clear. But they absolutely understand when some needs cannot be met. It's even better if you can explain why—budget restriction, company policy, legal issues, and so on. One mom I polled on this topic sent me a direct message to elaborate: "I'd be frustrated if my manager asked, I was told no, and they weren't willing to look for a compromise—but if there wasn't a reasonable compromise or there was a legitimate reason to say no, I would feel okay because it was a fair conversation."

This is a game-changing lesson in management of working moms: it is better to meaningfully ask working moms what they need and end up not being able to provide it, or to provide some lesser compromise, than it is to not ask them at all. Everyone I interviewed was overwhelmingly clear on this: moms want to "feel heard" or "be seen" by their managers. New moms feel supported just knowing that their manager cares enough to ask or demonstrates understanding about the challenging work–life juggle they are facing. That alone is support. Full-size fridge or not.

Fear of Playing Favorites

The pressure on managers to be fair to all the members on their team can be intense! Coincidentally, it can at times feel a bit like parenting. Managers tell me that concerns of playing favorites, either imagined or real, often stop them from showing support to working moms. Who wants to deal with the squabbling and resentment among your team? Most often, favoritism concerns come from employees who are not the working moms. *Why does that new mom get to work remotely for a month while the rest of us do not? I want a month off, too! She's always at the pediatrician with her kid, but I struggle to find time to fit my doctor's appointments in to our hectic schedule. Parents always get away with doing less, and we have to pick up the slack without recognition of our stress.* These are the kinds of concerns that I hear about, not only from manager colleagues but also, honestly, from my own peers as well in the years before we became parents.

Drawing a parallel between playing favorites and my parenting experience, I can tell you this: it is never possible to treat my two daughters equally. They aren't in the same situation. They are different ages and developmental stages. Here is a simple example: my oldest daughter receives more of the newly purchased clothing, and the youngest gets the hand-me-downs. They just aren't going to have an equal experience when it comes to new clothes because I am, like a manager, on a budget! However, as a parent, I work hard at practicing fairness. Not precisely equality, but fairness. While big sister gets newer clothes the most often, when younger sister decided to take up a sport with a significant requirement for uniforms and gear and equipment, we went for it. That sport was what mattered to her, and I gave her what she needed to do her special thing.

No, your childless workers are not going to get the identical supports as your new moms, who are possibly going through a different stage of life than those of other employees. But as managers, we should be listening to the needs of all our workers. Writers Joan C. Williams and Marina Multhaup argue in the *Harvard Business Review* that "if you give people time off work to run a marathon, you should give people time off work to take care of their sick kid. If you give people time off work because the nanny didn't show up again, you should give people time off work because their grandmother is sick."[4] Get ahead of or combat any claims of favoritism by asking your nonparent or parent-of-older-kid workers, "What do you need to succeed?" This is a great way to ward off tension between different groups of employees while creating an overall work culture of support. Everyone needs support; the support just looks different for different people, and employees must define that with you.

Belief That Personal Life Should Stay Personal

I am hoping I have made it clear that personal lives carry over heavily into work lives. But in case you or someone you work with are still holding on to this idea that personal and professional should stay separate, which is holding you back from communicating with working moms about support, let's dig further into the subject. Mental health is a prime example of how the personal runs right into the professional. The story of Patricia, the worker who had a medical emergency-level mental health breakdown in the office and whose story I shared in chapter one, clearly demonstrates that we cannot compartmentalize mental health in a way that keeps it out of the office. Work is such a huge part of our lives. It contributes to our mental health struggles, and

---

4. Joan C. Williams and Marina Multhaup, "How Managers Can Be Fair About Flexibility for Parents and Non-Parents Alike," *Harvard Business Review*, April 27, 2018, hbr.org/2018/04/how-managers -can-be-fair-about-flexibility-for-parents-and-non-parents-alike.

even if all the struggle is only coming from the personal side, such as a problem with a partner at home or a dying parent, there is no way to shut off that part of your brain while at work.

Mental health challenges are pervasive in the new-mom community. The type of mood and anxiety disorders experienced range widely and go beyond postpartum depression—we know now that new mothers experience everything from anxiety to depression to rage to psychosis and more. In fact, "suicide and overdose are the leading causes of death in the first year postpartum for new moms, with 100% of these deaths deemed preventable."[5] Mental health is a serious issue for moms and impacts their performance and functioning at work. There is no wall between mental health struggles at home and productivity at work. It's quite the opposite: mental health problems plague individuals and teams.

The data is staggering and shows that "employees with unresolved depression experience a 35% reduction in productivity, contributing to a loss to the US economy of $210.5 billion a year in absenteeism, reduced productivity,

---

5. "New Parents and Mental Health: Supporting Your Employees through the Most Common Complications of Pregnancy and Childbirth," Construction and Financial Management Association, accessed January 2, 2024, mass.cfma.org/articles/new-parents -and-mental-health-supporting-your-employees-through-the -most-common-complications-of-pre.

and medical costs."[6] The good news is that bringing mental health support into your office will not only benefit the working moms but also help all employees, of whom a quarter overall report feeling mental health challenges.[7]

Also, getting conversations about mental health out into the open at work might help *you*. Nearly 50 percent of managers and supervisors struggle with mental health disorders or significant stress-related conditions.[8] Turning this issue from *Leave mental health or other personal issues at home* to *We care about and support mental health at work* will make for a better workplace for everyone and result in better outcomes for your organization.

Of course, there is a need for personal and professional boundaries, which I will discuss more in chapter four, where we'll pull apart the reasons why new moms aren't speaking up for their needs. However, addressing issues of mental health, breastfeeding support, and transitioning back to work after a major life change like having a baby is fully appropriate for the workplace because these issues directly

6. "What Employers Need to Know About Mental Health in the Workplace," Mass General Brigham, accessed January 2, 2024, www.mcleanhospital.org/essential/what-employers-need-know -about-mental-health-workplace.

7. "What Employers Need to Know About Mental Health in the Workplace," Mass General Brigham.

8. "What Employers Need to Know About Mental Health in the Workplace," Mass General Brigham.

relate to your workers' productivity and success. Gossiping about your neighbor's affair in the office might be crossing the line of *Your personal life is personal*! But supporting new moms' mental health to bolster their success at work is not a personal topic—it is an everybody, everywhere topic. It's a management topic. It is time to change our thinking on this once and for all.

Every day, I ask working mothers on my team what they need, even though I have two kids of my own and operate a business that supports new moms, because every employee journey, every parenthood journey, every mental health journey, and every work–life balance journey is unique. I also like to manage in a place where I can be the real Sarah, even when I'm struggling myself as a person or as a boss.

Feeling Overwhelmed by Lack of Time

The struggle of not enough hours in the day to meet the abundance of tasks, deadlines, milestones, benchmarks, reports, meetings, and so forth is very real for us managers and leaders and small-business owners—and it might feel hard to think about finding the time to get these mom-support conversations in, plus following up and keeping tabs on how your team is doing on an ongoing basis. I get it. But in my experience, while investing in your team is a time commitment, it typically yields better long-term results: far fewer mistakes; a reduced incidence of overspending, complaints, mishaps, and liabilities; and better outcomes. I strongly recommend turning your attention toward long-term investment in working-mom employees over the short-term putting out of fires, such as the loss of employees, unhappy employees, and nonperforming employees. Here are a few strategies for managers who feel extremely limited on time and energy to work on building support:

1. Home in on simple communications that have the biggest bang for your buck. For example, send a text message to a new mom on maternity leave just to say, "How are you doing? Just wanted to check in and let you know we are wishing you well! If we can do anything to support you, please let me know." This can go a long way in creating feelings of support before the employee even comes back to work, getting you ahead of the communication curve. It will also save you time. Break the ice right away, get everything out on the table, and know as soon as possible if there is something needing discussion before they return to the office.

2. Whenever you talk with a working mom and they have a support request, consider getting them involved in doing some of the legwork, which will help you with sparse time. If the support needs require creative compromise like the kind my friend provided to her employee with the mini fridge,

consider asking your employee to do the research: *I like this idea, but I'm not really sure of the costs of a fridge or the different options. Could you research a variety of products from less expensive to more— or see what they are setting up like this in another department—and let me know so I can evaluate what would work with our budget? Bring back this information to me so we can keep the conversation going and find a solution.*

3. Leverage the casual time during your day so you don't have to add more meetings into your work schedule. Invite the working mom to lunch for the support conversation. Or if you are working remotely, send her a gift card for a coffee—seriously, caffeine is everything to a new mom—and have a fifteen-minute video chat. It is special to have this kind of time with your boss—it creates incredible goodwill and fits the conversation into your day in a time-efficient manner. Another idea: if you have a weekly meeting with this employee, spend five minutes at the start each time to check in on how things are going outside of the project or task list, such as her work schedule and mental health, the topics I have been covering here. This builds the support conversations into the regularly scheduled meetings.

4. Utilize other members of your team. I'm not suggesting you pass off the all-important *How can I*

support you? conversation to someone else, but you can ask other enthusiastic team players to help meet the needs. Specifically, are there any other new moms a little further along in their journeys who are interested in hosting an employee-focused new-parent lunch once a month to talk about personal and professional stressors and advice? If so, let them know that you would love to drop in for ten minutes at the beginning or end to hear what they are talking about and be a supporter. You will still need to engage, but you can enlist your colleagues to help carry some of the weight of getting people together in conversation. This is a great way to save yourself time while showing you care.

There are many reasons, some that may be unique to you, why managers do not initiate much or any conversation with the working moms on their teams. In this chapter, I've outlined some common reasons:

1. Lack of firsthand experience
2. Anxiety about liability, laws, and lawsuits
3. Worry about not being able to say yes
4. Fear of playing favorites
5. Belief that personal life should stay personal
6. Feeling overwhelmed by lack of time

The pressure on managers to meet goals and increase revenue while limiting spending and simultaneously supervising a dynamic group of people is immense; however, the reward of making the time, or finding time in efficient and creative ways, to better communicate with working moms is a win-win not only for your own manager happiness but also for aforementioned performance metrics.

4

Why Working Moms Aren't Asking for Support

I n this chapter, I will share with you the complex and numerous reasons why moms do not typically *initiate* conversations about support with their managers. So aptly put by award-winning journalist and author Amy Westervelt, society expects "women to work like they don't have children, and raise children as if they don't work."[1] Echoing this sentiment from my own experience as mom and manager, as well as from stories from other moms, I will share the ways in which working mothers are

---

1. Sheryl G. Ziegler, "How to Let Go of Working-Mom Guilt," *Harvard Business Review*, September 4, 2020, hbr.org/2020/09/how-to-let-go-of-working-mom-guilt?registration=success.

conditioned to believe that asking for help makes them less of a mother or employee—and how this stops them from being able to ask their managers for needed support. I will also discuss the tricky situation many moms face in keeping employment—a threat that is often cloaked in an unexpected promotion or a pivot in the job description instead of overt discrimination. Though sometimes, it is also just that.

My first reaction when I heard about the recent COVID-19 pandemic exodus of moms leaving the job force dubbed as the Great Resignation was that *resignation* was too neat of a word to use. *Resignation* is normally used to describe an empowered choice in a career. Like, "I put in a letter of resignation to pursue an opportunity at another organization." Instead, for most of these moms, the reality was "I cannot juggle zero childcare options and facilitate virtual learning while managing to do the same work in new conditions without increased support from my employer, so I am forced to quit." In my world, I'm renaming it: *Again, Moms Were Forced Out Because of Lack of Support.*

The ways in which we talk about moms being forced out of their jobs, because of mom responsibilities or support needs, tend to center heavily around it being a decision of motherhood over work: *She wanted to stay home with her baby.* This is not the case for many of these moms. Many of the moms in my surveys, polls, and interviews who had left previous jobs indicated that they could not remain in their jobs without support, even when they desperately wanted to keep those jobs or stay on their career paths.

Let's dive more in depth into the reasons mom aren't asking you for what they need. By the end of this chapter, you'll be convinced that silence from the new moms on your team does not mean they are doing okay; in fact, a lack of discussion about work–life balance and supportive policies and practices likely indicates a significant problem for the moms on your team.

I Will Lose My Job

Fear of losing their job is by far the biggest reason moms tell me they do not speak up. It's obvious: many families cannot afford to lose the income, moms like their jobs and want career advancement, and they feel that making a job move might be too challenging in the market or while having young kids. While you cannot legally fire employees for becoming pregnant if they can do the functions of their jobs, many moms tell me they know of another mom who was put on the mommy track and funneled into a lesser role, not by choice, but because they asked for flexibility or supports.[2] Or, conversely, they were given a huge new

2. "Fact Sheet: Pregnancy Discrimination," US Equal Employment Opportunity Commission, accessed January 2, 2024, www.eeoc .gov/laws/guidance/fact-sheet-pregnancy-discrimination.

workload that was not compatible with their immediate need for flexibility.

Several moms told me their experience of being pushed out of their jobs after returning from leave played out something a bit like this: *Welcome back from maternity leave. We're advancing the responsibility of your job now to travel three times a month and to take on this new project immediately that will require you to work extra hours.* Knowing the mom perspective here is enlightening in management; some moms feel backed into the corner of a ramped-up role soon after having a baby. Under the cover of a promotion or a change in the job description, they end up in roles they cannot sustain in the early months or years of parenting. They are dinged for "performance issues" after previously doing well in the job and given the exit card. They know they were pushed out.

When a mom knows at least one person in their sphere of friends and colleagues who has gone through something stressful like this—mommy track, workplace hostility, or being fired—they understandably become unwilling to rock the boat in their own jobs by asking for more help or support. When I surveyed moms about this issue, nearly 30 percent said that they don't ask their managers for help because they worry the managers will respond by adding more to their job descriptions to push them out of the roles. This is a real fear for many moms.

Assuming you are not actually pushing moms out of their jobs—or understand this is not good management practice and want to change—here are some ways you can create a workplace where moms do not worry about losing their jobs or being placed on the mommy track:

- Build a team culture where asking employees how they are doing is a regular occurrence. This is where we managers must really step up and act. When working moms see managers asking and not making assumptions on workload, opportunities for advancement, or what employees want and can handle, they are more likely to tell you when they need help.

- Build rapport and trust with the women and working moms on your teams. Throughout this book, I have offered many ideas for this: from being vulnerable and open about your own personal life to asking probing, thoughtful questions about your team members, to demonstrating your respect for employees' personal lives in your design of the schedule.

There is a multitude of ways to build trust. Some super simple ways to do this are to print out and pin a working-mom-relevant article to a bulletin board, send around an interesting link to your team about your company, or really anything else that makes sense for your team. You can, of course, do this for other topics, too, to make the working-mom piece stand out less and to address other important issues or fun topics that relate to employees. The news frequently covers issues related to working moms—it could, for instance, be the story of a mom who made some cool achievement in her job in another department that was featured internally or externally. I regularly send my teams links to articles such as "Innovative New Working-Mother Program at XYZ Company" or "Our State Ranks X in Working-Mother Supports." I then probe my team: "What do you think about this approach to scheduling? How do you feel about our state's ranking?" The point is to normalize talking about these issues and make it less scary for everyone to approach them. I often learn something important in doing this as well and put the interesting ideas or conversation into action on my team!

The Boss Will Never See Me the Same Again

Moms tell me that if they speak up to managers, they worry their bosses will see them as "the problem employee." These moms return to work after birth or adoption of a baby feeling hypersensitive, either because of the workplace culture or societal pressures—or both—that perceive their new difference as "less than" before.

These moms *do* feel different, so this presents a huge internal conflict at work. *We are changed after having a baby, but that does not make us less good at our jobs. How do we address the new support we need without being seen as needy?* It is hard for managers to navigate this experience for moms—we want moms to recognize and talk about the change, and hopefully ask them how they are doing and note their new needs, but we also know they do not want to be viewed as lesser because of the change. This tension is one of the top reasons I wrote this book. I want to help you bridge this information gap between manager and new mom so that you both reap the rewards of an improved workplace.

Amelia, a mom I spoke to about this topic, is in the legal department of a medical-device company. She shared with me the complex and confusing feelings about disclosing her motherhood journey to a manager:

> *It was so stressful going to doctors for so long without anyone knowing about it. We weren't sure if the in vitro fertilization (IVF) would be successful, and I didn't know how people would react knowing all the details. I was super uncomfortable about the idea of telling my boss, "I'm doing IVF, and it may or may not work—that's why I'm taking all this time off for appointments," knowing that the manager could start*

freaking out about me taking a maternity leave that might or might not happen.

Thankfully, I did get pregnant! I decided to use [my company's] generous maternity leave policy for sixteen weeks, but I knew I wouldn't return afterward. The work environment was toxic. They thought they were doing good for employees with the leave policy, which I do appreciate, but the culture was so bad, and I was afraid to talk to my boss. What I found interesting is that nobody ever explicitly said you could or could not have support; it was a feeling everyone had from the lack of supportive actions from the leadership. I think, if you asked my manager, she would say she is understanding and flexible, but she never talks to any of us employees about understanding or flexibility.

Two women employees who had babies before me did the same thing—they took the nice maternity-leave benefit and did not return at the end of leave. You would think my boss would figure out why people are doing this.

After I found a new job, I got pregnant again. I knew their maternity leave was much shorter (six weeks compared to sixteen at the previous job), and I took a pay cut when I moved to this job! But I chose to work here because they are supportive and outright about that. In the end, a strong maternity-leave policy is important, but ongoing support is what I need to stay and succeed at a job.

In Amelia's story, the misalignment between manager and moms regarding communication about support needs is profound. I was struck by her statement "I think, if you asked my manager, she would say she is understanding and flexible, but she never talks to any of us employees about understanding or flexibility." It is clear there is a huge disconnect between employees and manager in this case that could be addressed by open communication; instead, there are negative results that stem out of misunderstanding and the management practices in this organization.

Some moms speak up right away, finding themselves even more motivated than before they became parents to change their workplace for the better, either for themselves or other moms on their teams and those who come to their roles after them. But many moms, especially new moms in the first year after having a first child, do not yet feel empowered or in a safe space to ask their employers for what they need. One mom I spoke with said she wasn't even sure what she really needed right away; it took some time navigating new motherhood at work to identify her support needs, but she wished she could have had a conversation with her manager at the outset that kept the door open to ask. For this mom, if she'd had conversations with her manager, they wouldn't have started out in a straightforward way, like "I need a mini fridge for my pumped milk." Instead, it would have been more of a subtle back-and-forth with her manager on how things were going that would have eventually led to asking for support.

Here are some ways managers can normalize moms asking for support and make support needs something anyone on the team can discuss without fear of being seen as problematic:

- Create a culture of support that extends beyond working-mother support. An employee is more likely to share with you some of the challenges they are facing or the considerations they are weighing about staying in your organization if they feel comfortable talking with a manager before they even have children. For example, talk with all your employees regularly about work–life balance or mental health.

- Create safe spaces to talk about challenges and needs by sharing some of yours. On my team, I give glimpses into my own motherhood and life obstacles. For instance, I shared with my team when I was struggling mentally during the COVID-19 pandemic and when one of my kids was going through a particularly tough time, which was an indicator to the team—particularly, anyone being quiet about their life—that it was safe to talk to me.

- Create built-in opportunities to get feedback so that employees know there will be a structured opportunity to talk. Ask about working-mom support during performance reviews, maternity-leave transition planning, meetings about projects and tasks, and always during an exit interview.

Support Has an Expiration Date

One of the interesting topics that moms have spoken with me about is when managers or organizations "expire" their support for working moms; that is, they offer a nice benefit of support, but their policy, or even just personal tolerance for providing the support, wanes after a certain period of time. On the flip side, moms have also told me that they have not needed support or known what kind they needed right when they returned to work and later felt it was too late to ask for help. Moms have told me they get the feeling managers feel tired about providing support. Whether that is true or not, it is important for management to consider and reflect on how we approach working-mom support beyond the first conversations. I discussed in the introduction the importance of support to moms—and other parents—across the entire continuum of parenting. Ongoing conversations are important, as is regular reevaluation of benefits, policies, and other supports from the organization.

Let's look at this idea of "expired" support in more depth using the specific topic of breastfeeding. This is a topic where even the law (the PUMP Act) currently has a one-year end date, which you should know is misaligned with the American Academy of Pediatrics guidance that says moms should consider breastfeeding for two years or beyond.[3] Imagine the following: A company policy says its breastfeeding break time and space follows the federal law and thus is available for one year after the birth of a child. At this company, a breastfeeding working mom, encouraged by or perhaps feeling pressured by the evidence-based guidance given to them by their health providers, wants to feed breast milk for two years. How does the mom reconcile that? Perhaps if the mom asked their manager if they could keep using the lactation-room benefit beyond a year, it would be an easy yes. But if the policy says a year, it is easy to understand why a mom would be hesitant to talk to their manager for additional support. The working mom is faced with asking for a change to a written policy and might worry that they will stand out to the human resources department or to their boss as being different, maybe even problematic. The mom could feel like this is

_____

3. Alyson Sulaski Wyckoff, "Updated AAP Guidance Recommends Longer Breastfeeding Due to Benefits," American Academy of Pediatrics News, June 27, 2022, publications.aap.org/aapnews/news /20528/Updated-AAP-guidance-recommends-longer.

asking for special treatment. But they may also really want to achieve their goals and do what moms are being told is optimal for the health of their babies. Such an internal conflict! Maybe the mom is worried that the conversation with a manager will be awkward, questioned, or judged: "Why do you need to breastfeed for that long?" And what if the mom does speak up and ask the manager for more lactation support and the manager says no? Does that mean the mom has to end their breastfeeding journey because now everyone is scrutinizing why they are taking a break time? Or will the mom have to start sneaking around to pump? At the end of this section, I'll give you some manager tips on how to help address expired support. It's a real pressure on the working moms on your team.

I host a "Mental Health Monday" question-and-answer event for the moms in my network, with the answers provided by a licensed independent clinical social worker whom I added to my team. Every month, at least one person, if not several, asks, "Can postpartum depression or anxiety show up months after my baby is born? I did not struggle with this before, but my baby is nine months old, and now I feel sad." The clinical answer is yes. I think most people, moms included, believe postpartum is only the six weeks or so after a baby is born or until the mom gets the "all-clear" from her OB-GYN, or maybe it lasts for the months we qualify as newborn (0–3 months) for the baby, that "fourth trimester" period. Did you know that, medically speaking, the third phase of postpartum lasts up to six months?[4] And newer research has shown that postpartum depression can occur all the way up to a year after birth—as in, a mom can feel fine coming back to work after leave, operate without depression for months in the office, and then experience PPD. In a small percentage of cases, PPD can last up to three years.[5]

This information matters to you as manager. It is important to know and realize in the support you provide that a positive, upbeat, successful first week back at the office after baby is not an indicator of how a mom is doing for their entire mom experience. Support needs to be ongoing, without a defined end. This does not mean benefits have to be limitless; as a manager, I understand the need to be clear on policies and procedures and mindful of budgets, but it is important to evaluate the costs or resources against the implications for the moms on your team and their desire and ability to stay in their role.

Here are some ways you can address "expired support" on your teams:

---

4. Mattea Romano, Alessandra Cacciatore, Rosalba Giordano, et al., "Postpartum Period: Three Distinct but Continuous Phases, *Journal of Prenatal Medicine* 4, no. 2 (April 2010): 22–25, www .ncbi.nlm.nih.gov/pmc/articles/PMC3279173/.

5. "Postpartum Depression May Last for Years," National Institutes of Health, November 10, 2020, www.nih.gov/news-events/nih -research-matters/postpartum-depression-may-last-years.

- Evaluate to see if your organization's policies for working-mom support have "end dates." If so, are those end dates grounded in an important reason for the company, or are they arbitrary? Did someone developing this policy just say one year is the limit on use of the pumping room because that's what the law required or because it sounded reasonable? Remember: federal laws are the "minimum" protections and not necessarily the best practice! Would you automatically give every team member minimum wage in an organization trying to be competitive? No, probably not. The same is true of federally required minimums for other work policies, like breastfeeding. You can give someone a fridge even if the law doesn't say you must. Maybe your company does not even really care how long the lactation room is utilized; someone just stuck a date on it. Revisit these policies.

- Evaluate whether managers, leaders, and your colleagues are aware that postpartum health conditions can occur significantly later than the new mom's first weeks or months back at work. Remember how I talked in a previous section about sharing interesting articles with your team that normalize working-mom (and other kinds of employee) support? Postpartum depression would be a perfect subject matter to share with your organization to help everyone understand that this is not a black-and-white, now-or-never issue.

- Evaluate whether you've left the door open in a thoughtful, welcoming way for the working mothers on your team to come ask for help on an ongoing basis. Do the working moms know they can come to you, particularly when they are nearing the end of a benefit they still need access to? Overtly tell them: "You can come to me at any time, meaning any time now or in the distant future, if you are having a challenge and need to talk about solutions."

Everyone Else Has Figured This Out

One of the most frequently asked questions I receive in my weekly ask-me-anything session is "How do you juggle work and motherhood so well, Sarah?" I find this question terribly difficult to answer, mainly because I worry that the new moms who follow my social media think I am out and about in the world having completely figured out work–life balance. So much of how we navigate work and motherhood is unique to our family and our job, and what works for me might not be the same for another mom, which is why managers need to ask moms instead of following one pathway of support.

And, social media, while a great place to get mom support, also perpetuates this feeling of mom inadequacy. In fact, studies have shown that most younger mothers are engaging in motherhood content on social media nearly every day of the week for several hours a day. When they do this, they "begin comparing themselves to the people around them and making self-judgments. These self-evaluations can lead to negative feelings, particularly when they stem from upward social comparisons—comparisons to people who seem better off than oneself."[6] Researchers have found that moms have a negative physical response—releasing stress hormones—to all this comparing and worrying about being "mom enough."

So I tell my mom followers, yes, I am successful in business, and I am my own boss, which is truly a benefit to my work–life balance. I also have so much privilege: house cleaning, childcare when the girls were little, an engaged partner, mental health resources to work through struggles. But I, too, lack the instruction manual or magic bullet for work–life balance that we all wish existed. When I had my first baby, I did not speak up and ask for help when I needed it. I struggled with mom guilt and career guilt—I was overwhelmed and exhausted. At the time, I led a nonprofit organization

_____

6. Beth Ellwood, "Mothers Who Spend More Time on Social Media Sites About Motherhood Experience Higher Stress Hormone Levels, Study Finds," PsyPost: Social Psychology, November 2, 2022, www.psypost.org/mothers-who-spend-more-time-on-social-media -sites-about-motherhood-experience-higher-stress-hormone-levels -study-finds/.

and felt pressured to hold a steady presence for everyone. But for me, as it is for all working moms, it was—and still is—trial and error. Test and learn. Fall and get back up. I rarely apply 100 percent effort at work and family at the same time—I don't have 200 percent capacity. I love talking about these topics, clearly, but I worry when moms believe that everyone else has their sh——t together when they do not.

Silence about support in the workplace culture is a huge contributor to this false sense new moms have that everyone else is okay. Motherhood is isolating as it is; allowing a culture of silence about new motherhood in the workplace most certainly creates more isolation, stress, and anxiety for the moms on your team, even if they have good poker faces. Moms tell me that when other moms on the team are quiet, they don't believe they are suffering—they believe they have it all figured out without help. That's what social media tells them. And social media is often one of the few places moms are engaging with other moms.

Here's how can you help moms feel less inadequate and know that it is okay to try and learn, pivot, and change course to figure out a pathway for their work–life balance that will promote the highest level of success.

- Focus your outreach on more than just the struggling mom. Don't forget to ask the most "put together" and highest-achieving working mothers on your team how they are doing, too. You may have to probe extra hard to pull information out of these moms, since their tendency is to gloss things over from the pressure of societal norms and self-expectations. When it comes to mental health, you may have seen the memes to "check on your strong friend." The same is true for your employees. Check on your "perfectly fine" new mom and make sure they are really okay.

- Focus on facilitating parents across your team to get together for sharing and support. It is nearly impossible for working mothers—and other parents—to hang out after work. Moms tell me they are so lonely and isolated in the beginning of parenthood. Perhaps you can dedicate a little bit of work time to this each month; set up a once-a-month fifteen-minute coffee break, parent lunch time, or Zoom event. Call it a task force, working group, or meetup, provide the group with a small coffee budget, protect the bit of time for the moms and other parents to meet, and offer to be a part of it. (Or not—let them have their space, too.) Consider saying, "I support the space and time for the parent meetup, and I'd like you to know that I would love to be invited if there is ever anything I should hear or could support you on, but it is also okay for it to be parents only."

- Focus on ways you can connect with your working-mom employees to make them feel less alone or inadequate, even if you don't share the parenting experience. Stating that you value work–life balance and demonstrating that through your own actions, such as taking time off and knowing when to disconnect, will send the message. The working moms I talked with in writing this book say that having specific examples of how you relate are not necessary—you don't have to be a mom or know a mom—but using a tone that expresses the importance of having a happy life outside of work will demonstrate your empathy.

Parenting Intensely (and Without Help) Is the Only Way

The oldest of Gen Z are becoming parents and demonstrating a parenting intensity unlike that of previous generations—more hands-on involvement in the daily lives of their kids and higher perfectionism goals aimed for than their millennial predecessors in the workforce right now. This next generation of parents who will over the next few years fully staff up our teams are completing higher educational levels while beginning to juggle the demands of parenthood. And a recent study showed that 83 percent of Gen Z parents believe it is important to be a "perfect" mom, compared to 77 percent of millennial parents and even smaller percentages in older generations.[7] The intensity of work and family life is increasing in ways we have not experienced before on our teams.

The capacity of working mothers is nothing short of amazing—remember the business case I made for wanting these incredible moms on your teams—but, no, they are not superhuman, and to expect them to be so is a recipe for disaster. Psychologists have even discovered a correlation between the quest for "perfect motherhood" and severe burnout, proving the whole "perfect" concept is a disaster, with findings suggesting that "intensive mothering norms might have severe costs for women's family and work outcomes."[8] Supporting these moms as managers and creating connections between parents in your workplace is becoming more important than ever before to avoid the potential of burnout at work.

The intensity expectations are not just among moms; they are growing as part of our work culture, too. Amelia,

---

7. Caroline Picard, "Gen Zers and Millennials Have Very Different Ideas of What It Means to Be the 'Perfect Parent,'" What to Expect, February 16, 2023, www.whattoexpect.com/news/first-year/gen-z-millennials-perfect-parent.

8. Loes Meeussen, and Colette Van Laar, "Feeling Pressure to Be a Perfect Mother Relates to Parental Burnout and Career Ambitions," *Frontiers in Psychology* 9 (November 2018): 2113, doi.org/10.3389/fpsyg.2018.02113.

whose story I recounted earlier in this chapter, shared a practice at her previous job that had intense expectations for the team to be always "on." The remote workers at her company were required to keep their online work chat light green; they were not to let the chat status fall to idle yellow—while, say, walking the dog or managing a personal call—or the boss would think they were not performing. Side note, to validate Amelia's rigorous chat-light expectations, I came across an advertisement for—and I am not kidding you—a robotic tool that moves your computer mouse to keep you in active status if you forget to move the mouse manually! Before Amelia had kids, she said the chat-light rule was mostly just annoying, not a deal-breaker. However, when she became pregnant, she could not envision juggling "keep the light green" with being a new mom. What if the pediatrician called about an appointment and she forgot to wiggle her computer mouse? Or because of lack of sleep, she forgot to keep the chat active even when she was on the phone with a colleague? She could not manage the mental health stress of being intensely "on" at work while also being intensely "perfect" as a mom. She would have to make a job change. My own youngest daughter did not sleep through the night fully until she was ten months old—I was deep back into my work before I was getting adequate rest where I would have remembered to wiggle my mouse while reading a report.

Amelia's story is not an indication that working mothers cannot both have successful careers and be moms; what it exposes is the toxic methodologies used by some work-places to measure performance with no consideration for the employee on the other end. Strong management takes engaged conversation and cannot be achieved by a game of red-light/green-light chat status. Amelia's employer lost a high-performing employee to another organization that supports Amelia and checks on her rather than her chat light.

It is not surprising that the rates of diagnosed anxiety or depression, or both, for working moms with small children exceed 40 percent.[9] Here's how one mom described this stress: "I want to show my coworkers that I can continue to effectively handle a high quantity of work despite the restraints of childcare. I want to prove to other parents I know that I have the time and energy to dedicate myself to my family and my child's development and that work won't take me away from it."[10] As a mom myself, I absolutely feel this; I am simultaneously amazed at the incredible resilience and resourcefulness of moms—again, you want these people on your teams. But, wow—I also wonder: When will the well run dry for moms? Mary Beth Ferrante, a *Forbes* contributor and advocate for inclusive workplaces, says,

---

9. "The Mental Health Crisis of Working Moms," CVS Health and Harris Poll, October 25, 2022, www.cvshealth.com/news/mental-health/the-mental-health-crisis-of-working-moms.html.

10. "The Pressure Society Puts on Working Moms Isn't OK—Here's Why," The Everymom, August 23, 2019, theeverymom.com/pressure-society-puts-on-working-moms-isnt-ok/.

"[Moms] will only be successful if employers and managers who shape office policy and work culture support them in all aspects of their life, at home and at work."[11] As a manager, it is important to note that the next generation also has expectations that their bosses and workplace culture will recognize the importance of the successful family and personal life they desire. We will have to respond to this.

When you combine the social media and self-imposed pressure to be the perfect mom with an intensity at work to be an always-on employee, plus fears about speaking up about this untenable balance, your working moms will struggle and might leave. My hope is that through what I'm sharing in these pages, managers will gain a broader understanding of and reach out to the current and future generations of parents. These employees grew up watching and comparing themselves on social media; they were then isolated in their early parenting or coming-of-age years during the COVID-19 pandemic and are now putting a tremendous amount of pressure on themselves.

Here are some ways you as a manager can help support incoming generations of mom employees who come with a perfectionist perspective on parenting:

---

11. Mary Beth Ferrante, "The Pressure Is Real for Working Mothers," *Forbes*, August 27, 2018, www.forbes.com/sites/marybeth ferrante/2018/08/27/the-pressure-is-real-for-working-mothers/?sh =8fb67772b8f6.

- Demonstrate that performance is measured not by the process used to get the job done but by end results, allowing employees with different flexibility needs, generational values, perspectives, and personal life demands to excel. I think it is safe to say most managers are not watching the chat-status light like Amelia's manager was, so putting that aside, consider where you might have limiting ways of measuring performance on your team. Extroverts, introverts, morning people, night owls, standing-desk lovers, coffee shop workers, mothers—they all get the job done differently. Embrace different paths to success.

- Demonstrate that you are open-minded and enjoy hearing about different parenting styles, generations, cultures, and ways of thinking. One mom in my network told me that she knew her manager wanted to have kids and was struggling with fertility challenges, so this mom did not feel comfortable asking for what she needed from her boss. If you are open about some aspect of your life that might impede a mom speaking up about her life, keep that in mind and make space for her needs, too. This would go for parenting styles as well; be mindful of what you say about parenting so that it doesn't result in self-judgment for the moms on your team, hindering them from speaking up for their own unique needs (e.g., avoid throwing out lines like "Back in my day, we didn't breastfeed at work").

- Demonstrate your own vulnerabilities. Whether that is tossing into a meeting how you spilled your coffee on the drive in—been there, done that—and forgot to call your mother to wish her a happy birthday, or something more profound, like sharing your own health struggles, demonstrate vulnerability to your teams so they have a safe space to do the same. They may think a lack of vulnerability on your part means you really have the perfect life and leadership role, without a stress in the world, when I would guess that is not the case. I am very open with my own team; I do not write generic "Appointment" to block out time on the team calendar, I write "Sarah Therapy Appointment." You may not be comfortable with that in the way that I am, but I challenge you to be vulnerable to some extent with your teams. You normalize vulnerability for everyone else, and in turn, it takes the edge off for your employees who feel like they have to be perfect.

We Won't Connect on This Topic

Another time in which working mothers feel hesitant to speak up to their managers is when they feel awkward just bringing up topics like fertility, pregnancy, breastfeeding, and mental health. Moms tell me this might be because a manager is a different gender, or not a parent themselves, or has expressed challenges with becoming a parent as mentioned in the previous section. Moms have the same concerns as many of you managers do about connecting with each other! Coworkers and colleagues struggle with this, too. Everyone is a little uneasy talking about these topics with each other, especially if they don't have firsthand experience. It is going to take your initiative here to break the ice. I will help you with that in chapter six!

In my research for this book, I noticed a trend among online resources and books for new moms in how to approach their managers about their support needs: there is an undertone in nearly all this guidance of *Don't say too much! Give your manager time to absorb this news*—as if you just told them that someone died. *Know your rights and the retaliation process beforehand. Expect your manager not to be happy.* There are many great supportive managers who would be excited for an employee's exciting pregnancy announcement, so kudos to them—and no stereotypes here from me, but if I were a first-time mom reading this preparatory guidance, I would be so scared! While an employee shouldn't expect their boss to care about their pregnancy announcement at the level their friends and family do, and they should have questions about the job implications, the unhelpful and, perhaps, unnecessary vibe of "managers hate pregnancies" still persists, even in the mom literature.

Recapping from chapter three, where I discussed this topic from the manager perspective, now that we know that moms share similar awkward feelings or fears about bringing up support topics, here are some conversation starters for managers that may help encourage moms to feel more comfortable speaking about these issues:

- *If you decide to breastfeed, I want you to know we offer XYZ lactation benefits and will support you in your journey.* See what I did there? You are not having to ask if they are going to breastfeed—I get that this is awkward and sensitive for many. The mom may respond, "Thank you, I appreciate that," and that could be the end of what you hear on this subject, indicating they do not want to share more or that they may tell you more later. Either way, you have shown support and opened the door.

- *I'm new to a lot of these topics and do not know much about [IVF, pregnancy, breastfeeding, mental health, etc.], but I would like to know more about how I could support you. I am available if you are comfortable sharing.*

- *I would like to be better informed about what you are going through. Is there a link to a good resource site that you could send me so I could understand a bit more?* This is also a great way as a manager to buy yourself a little time to absorb what your employee has said.

I'm Asking for Too Much

When a mom can see or feel that your organization would struggle to meet their needs, they often do not ask for them. This could be due to obvious understaffing or limited financial resources, or even a job industry where flexibility is difficult—I am thinking of one of my customers who is a firefighter and uses a wearable breast pump while driving the fire truck because emergencies cannot wait for pump breaks and firefighters are not always near the designated pump space. It is great that these moms are being sensitive to your needs as manager or organization, but you still do not want to lose them to organizations that can offer them more adequate support.

In the last chapter, you heard about my friend and how she figured out how to provide a fridge for breast milk in the office with limited resources. When I polled moms about this topic, the vast majority said a compromise on support is totally okay and that the most important thing is a show of support. One mom said, "If it is clear that my manager has exhausted all of their resources and cannot do more, I understand that." Here are a few pointers on how to address a situation with a new mom when it is apparent the organization cannot offer all of the support that might be requested or needed:

- Get creative! I mean, *really* creative. Do you know how many mini fridges college students offload on freecycle groups and Facebook Marketplace? I just looked at my own local marketplace, and there were over two hundred smaller refrigerators listed for way under fifty dollars and a handful listed for free.
- When financial resources are tough, amp up the no-cost flexibility options like work-from-home, schedule flexibility, and time off for appointments. We always did this in my previous nonprofit organizations; our pay was lower in ratio to the education and skills of the staff, and our benefits were lean, but our flexibility was outstanding.
- Talking is free. Talk a lot with your employees about their situations—talking is support. Utilize my previous ideas for getting employees to talk to each other both as positive peer support and to take a load off of your time if you feel pressured.
- Ask guest speakers to come in and chat with your team about work–life balance, mental health, and so on. You may find lots of free community resources for this.

- When flexibility is challenging to offer, like for my customer who is a firefighter or for an active-duty mom or a frontline health worker, find unique ways to meet their support needs. Provide a small budget for a cooler bag and ice pack for the mom riding on the fire truck. Make sure the organization's mental health supports are available via telehealth and aren't just in-person counselor services, such as for a nurse who works the night shift and needs greater flexibility for appointments. Acknowledge and validate the challenge of balancing it all in your unique industry.

Through this chapter, you have learned that asking for help is a challenge for a lot of working mothers and why this is the case. Here are some of the key reasons moms are not speaking up:

1. I will lose my job.
2. The boss will never see me the same again.
3. Support has an expiration date.
4. Everyone else has this figured out.
5. Parenting intensely (and without help) is the only way.
6. We won't connect on this topic.
7. I'm asking for too much.

The stress of working-mom guilt is everywhere and well documented. Sheryl G. Ziegler, a therapist, said in the *Harvard Business Review*, "Instead of asking for help, a working mom may just be fueling her stress by trying to do it all herself—then realizing that it is just impossible. Asking for help takes practice, but once you take a vulnerable step in doing so, others around you will start doing the same."[12]

I hope as a manager that you now understand that most moms need support, and rarely do they need none. We have also learned that not hearing any requests from moms is not an accurate measurement of working-mom success on your teams. In the conclusion of this book, I will share with you my vision for the ultimate supportive workplace, where managers initiate support and moms are empowered to speak up for their needs. In that scenario, the communication flows easily and often as it becomes sustainable in your work culture, and the pressure on you as a manager begins to lift as communication and support just become a routine part of team culture, taking up a lot less of your time! In the meantime, if you are not quite there yet, utilize this newfound knowledge about the internal challenges working mothers face to make the first move toward support.

---

12. Ziegler, "How to Let Go of Working-Mom Guilt," *Harvard Business Review*.

5

Best Practices for Communication with Working Moms

There's that old saying that you don't know what you have until it's gone. When the COVID-19 pandemic hit, suddenly, our people connections vanished. As a result, mental health suffered for millions around the globe as we craved the kind of communication and engagement we once had. This sudden shift directly impacted managers, who had to scramble to find unique ways to keep teams rolling forward in a much tougher work atmosphere. We adapted using technology, but it was never quite the same as before. In the months and years following the return to work, in one form or another, many managers, including me, experienced a changed workforce—people who had spent a lot of time at home reconsidering what they wanted in life. Many of our team members left their jobs, even their careers, moved cities, or ended or started personal and professional relationships. The pandemic has had significant implications for how we manage employees who have different expectations about engagement than they had in the decades before.

In my industry, in-person trade shows where brands exhibited products and services to potential customers were long gone or facing attendance issues by 2019, with social media and digital advertising taking over as the modality of connection. Yet, since 2022, I've seen a resurgence of trade shows; trade show organizers who'd hung up their hats for years are suddenly back with new and more events. With so much advanced technology to reach customers, it's interesting to think about why we're reverting to expensive in-person events. I think the reason is because we deeply missed those human connections— and savvy organizations are capitalizing on this. Similarly, managers wanting to recruit and retain top talent on their teams have seen and will see that delivering this human connection is critical to success going forward. And I do not mean simply bringing people back to work in-person in an office. I mean engagement with your team, wherever they are. Generation Z, whom I discussed in previous chapters, *expect* human connections at work and will take jobs based on this level of engagement and support and avoid employers that do not offer it. Ravi Swaminathan, a business coach who regularly works with young new members of the workforce, wrote for *Fast Company* that "[Gen Z] expect authentic leadership and human connection, and they need robust training and leadership programs . . . Smart employers appreciate these distinct characteristics and will craft relevant employee experience offerings—from career coaching to mental health."[1]

Gratefully, technology does allow us to tap into meetings that once took two days of travel—and time away from family—to attend, and I believe we do not want to move back from those advancements and flexibilities. Most of the moms I talk to see remote work and increased independence from the office as a huge support to their work–life balance. However, employees, especially the up-and-coming generations of talent, are prioritizing connection and engagement with their managers and colleagues in a way that makes them *feel* something about the job they are doing. Engagement might be as simple as a boss who demonstrates active listening and appreciation. One mom told me that "the pandemic put into perspective what really matters to

---

1. Ravi Swaminathan, "The Four Crucial Expectations Gen Z Teams Have for the Workplace," Fast Company, September 14, 2022, www.fastcompany.com/90784200/the-4-crucial-expectations-gen-z-teams-have-for-the-workplace.

me, and that I must take charge of my career to make that happen. I feel more empowered now to change jobs if my current job doesn't meet my expectations." Another mom shared: "After so much time at home with family the last few years, I realized that any time away from my family has to be spent with people who actually care about me." I believe that your working moms—and many other team members—crave this engagement at work, and your future hires will demand it.

Plan to Engage

Strongly written human resources policies; robust diversity, equity, and inclusion initiatives; top-tier employee-benefits programs; and flexible scheduling all make for better teams and organizations. But without manager engagement of employees—and by that, I mean intentional, planned, strategic connections—organizations will fail. The industries and organizations that are on the cutting edge know that making connections is how to attract top-tier customers, clients, and talent. Caitlin Duffy, a research director at Gartner, a strategic advising firm for companies, says: "The intent to leave or stay in a job is only one of the things that people are questioning as part of the larger human story we are living . . . . You could call it the 'Great Reflection.'" She points to three core areas that employees demand in the next chapter of the workforce:

1. Employees are people, not just workers.
2. Work is a subset of life, not separate from it.
3. Value comes through feelings, not just features.[2]

From here, I'm going to break down "engaged communication" with working moms into a few areas of consideration before you dive deep into conversations with new moms on your teams. My goal is to fully equip you as manager to excel in your communications with working moms; this requires understanding what good communication sounds and looks like. In chapter six, we'll get into the specifics on how to start these conversations.

Develop Your Questions

In the previous chapter, you learned that most new moms are afraid to speak up and tell you what they need, so it is paramount that you sharpen your question-asking skills. Likely, as a manager, you are already aware of the types of questions you cannot ask legally, or of questions that, while not explicitly illegal, can demonstrate an intent to discriminate, which *is* illegal. To recap, these questions include, but are not limited to, the following:

---

2. Jordan Turner, "Employees Seek Personal Value and Purpose at Work. Be Prepared to Deliver," Gartner, March 29, 2023, www.gartner.com/en/articles/employees-seek-personal-value-and-purpose-at-work-be-prepared-to-deliver.

- Do you have children?
- When do you plan to have children?
- Who will take care of your children when you're at work?
- How old are your children?
- Are you pregnant?
- Do you plan on getting pregnant again?[3]

Think about which questions you can or should ask that get to the crux of support needs while avoiding any kind of bias or judgment, and then add these great questions to your manager toolkit. Learning to ask informed and meaningful questions will become the basis for your successful communication. Consider the following in your manager communications with new moms:

- Questions that identify workplace issues and log-jams for new moms, such as gaps in technology for successful remote-work performance or inadequate scheduling for flexible work. Think back to that example where the mom who worked in a bank could not feasibly commute to daycare before it closed for the day because of her work end time.

---

3. "Pregnancy Discrimination—FAQs," US Equal Employment Opportunity Commission, accessed January 2, 2024, www.eeoc .gov/youth/pregnancy-discrimination-faqs#Q10.

These are the logistical questions you want to get at in conversations with the new moms on your team.

- Questions about career, performance, and duties as they relate to the employee's aspirations—yes, moms still have career aspirations! Keep checking in about these and ask whether they want more responsibility or how they think projects or tasks are going. Just because an employee becomes a mom does not mean they suddenly have lowered their aspirations to achieve at work. Make no assumptions.

- Questions about mental health that remain open-ended for new moms to take the conversation as far as they feel comfortable and as often as they need to. We know from research and experience that employees without mental health support cannot succeed in your organization and that challenges in this area are rampant. Examples might include the following: "How do you feel about your work–life balance at the company right now?" "How can I support you without overstepping?" "Do you feel you have the right amount of workload right now, or are you overwhelmed?"

- Questions about the community of support around the employee, such as what childcare options are available in the community or whether they feel isolated at work and would benefit from connection to other employees on their parenthood journey.

- Questions that probe beyond the day-to-day issues and think one step ahead for the employee. For example, one mom recently told me that while her organization has an adequate space for using a breast pump in the office, there were no accommodations at a large conference venue she was required to attend. What is coming up on the employee's work agenda in the next few months, and how could you get ahead of providing support by asking about that now?

In chapter six, I will give you conversation prompts specific to new moms and share examples from real workplace stories that will help you zero in on the questions you want to ask. For now, start thinking categorically on the question themes relevant to your organization. Likely, just from reading the bullet points above, you have already thought of an area of "questioning" with moms on your team you had not considered before.

Be Ready to Ask Again—and Again

What works today for a new mom might be completely irrelevant by tomorrow. For a new parent, that 9 AM to 5 PM in-person schedule at the office is going along just fine, and then the daycare closes for a two-week spring break in April, and the mom must piece together a mishmash of support from family and a neighbor on a different schedule and routine. As a manager, perhaps you could offer temporary remote work or a revised start or end time, or both, to your employee's schedule. That would be a lifesaver for a couple of weeks, ensuring continuity on a project and reduced workplace stress. Some support, like for this example of a daycare closure, is short-term and temporary.

The support plan you work out with a mom on your team before they take maternity leave or when they come back after leave likely needs to be revisited on an ongoing basis. Your continued questions to new moms are critical to keeping the lines of communication open to reduce the chance of anyone being blindsided by a change or lack of reliability on your team. What new moms say they want and need to be successful on the job in the early postpartum days is unlikely to be the final word as their children's needs change, a partner's support or schedule is modified, a family member suffers illness, a breastfeeding journey ends, or childcare services fall through. Most new moms will tell you one day they feel like they have it all figured out, and the next they start over again from scratch; the only thing consistent about having kids is that every day is different. Keep the lines of communication open and keep the questions coming.

It is not just the arrangements for the kiddos or the needs of a child that change; moms change along the way, too. When a new mom on your team tells you that she is happy with her workload right now and is fine to hold off taking on new projects, this may not still be the case months later. So do not assume you should never again give her interesting and challenging new tasks until the kid is off to college. The worst thing a manager can do is make assumptions about new moms and what they want for their job or workload. Keep asking. The more you ask, the more in sync you'll be with your team and know where they stand.

Develop and Demonstrate Empathy

Can you *learn* to be empathetic to new mom employees? Yes, absolutely! Even if you think you are already an empathetic manager, I encourage you to work on developing empathy with new moms, who might need or appreciate it in a different form from other employees. Read on in this section for the types of empathy moms are looking for and how to demonstrate empathy as a manager—you can also even find empathy training in formal management continuing-education programs. It is to be expected that you will not relate to all the experiences of your employees, and diversity of experience and perspective is a great benefit to organizations. You may not have the same gender, race, cultural background, sexual orientation, educational background, or parenthood status as that of your employees, but that does not mean you cannot demonstrate empathy to people different from you.

When it comes to new moms, most say the same thing to me in discussion of this topic: *empathy for working moms is validation.*

Managers can validate the moms on their teams by approaching conversations and topics in an *affirmative* way: that is, by believing the moms and the experiences and stress they are going through whether or not you share in those experiences. For example, when one of my team member's work availability and stress levels were impacted by a multitude of illnesses among her kids, I started the conversation with "It must be so difficult right now to see your children so sick. I was sorry to hear about this and wanted to see if there was anything I could do to help support you with the projects on your list this week." This team member did not need anything work related from me in this conversation, but she did vent about the pressure she had been under at home and thanked me for observing that this was a hard time. I noticed that after this conversation, her attentiveness to her projects perked up, and we had a steady stream of progress updates from there.

Empathy in communication with new moms on your team unfolds in several ways:

- By demonstrating that you are a human with vulnerabilities just like the moms—and other employees—on your team. If you are a parent, talk about it. You could lead with something like "I remember how

often kids get sick and how stressful that can be."
If you are not a parent, talk about those things that
inevitably challenge you in your personal life. I
mentioned in a previous chapter that I talk openly
with my team about going to therapy for anxiety. It
sends the signal: *the boss makes herself vulnerable
to us, so she'll be empathetic when we do the same.*

- By keenly observing what's going on in the day-to-
day lives of your moms. In some workplaces, you
might see or hear about this during casual-type
talk about what's going on in everyone's lives. If
people don't share as openly, it might come out
on the work-productivity side, so the conversation
might start more broadly, like "Are there any challenges you are facing right now that I might help
you address?" One mom I surveyed said, "Managers
need to understand that everyone has something
going on even if it it's not apparent."
- In addressing the challenges with responsive solutions. The moms I surveyed for this book said
that the bulk of the support they need comes just
through a manager asking about it. And then, offering solutions can be a great next step. Whether your
ideas and implementation are through changes to
workplace policies or practices, or by providing
services or creating more avenues for new moms to
talk with each other, empathy is demonstrated by

listening to how new moms answer the questions you ask and demonstrating in your actions that they have been heard.

Again, even if you think you are already empathetic, I encourage you to take a step back and evaluate your skills in this area. Studies have shown that only 40 percent of managers are skilled in empathy.[4] Bravo if you are in that group, but in case you find yourself like the majority of managers who need to plan for and develop empathy with their teams, this is your jumping-off point to do just that. To conclude, one of the absolute best ways to demonstrate empathy in your communications with all employees, new moms included, is to be an intentional question asker and listener.

Choose Timing Wisely and Aim for Clarity

Recently on my own team's remote chat platform, I was sharing profound results from some successful new product launches, largely attributed to the hard work of my team. We were celebrating and sending out virtual high-fives and all the fun memes, and then I realized one of the

---

4. Verity Creedy and Scott Wolf, "How Leading with Emotional Intelligence Drives Engagement," DDI, June 2020, www .ddiworld.com/blog/leading-with-emotional-intelligence-drives -engagement.

key players in that success was not on the clock then, as she works a flex schedule that had coincided with her daycare availability. I had already let the cat out of the bag in my release of the good news, so it was too late to retract. But it was a good wake-up call for me: timing is everything in making moms feel included and validated. Even when it comes to good news!

Having good timing is key to effective delivery of your communication as a manager. It is logical to take into consideration the mood of the person and the environment before delivering bad news or to warm up a conversation before diving into something complex. But timing is also important for exciting opportunities, team celebrations, and even just plain fun when it comes to supporting working moms. Thoughtful actions speak volumes to working moms on our teams; when there is something monumental to share, good or bad, to the best of your ability take into consideration whether your timing is respectful of the flexibility or arrangement you have set up with your working moms. This demonstrates that you fully embrace the support you have offered, and it respects agreed-upon boundaries.

In chapter six, I will share the concept of creating a transition plan with the working moms—or soon-to-be moms—on your team. Tying this into timing, another consideration in managing moms is being aware that many first-time parents have absolutely no idea what they need until they need it. So, while I'm a huge proponent of advanced and planned communications with working moms, keep in mind that you may not get much of an answer when you ask questions in starter conversations and may need to revisit the questions at a different time. You can ask an employee if they want to use the lactation room when they return to work after leave, but they could be unsure whether they will be breastfeeding then. Or you may offer support in the way of flexible work schedule, but they might need to get back to you after they look at a partner's schedule, a baby's sleep schedule, their commute, and other factors.

Another important component for successful communication with working moms is clarity in exactly what you need and by when. There is no time in my life thus far where I have been fuzzier mentally than in the first weeks or months after my daughters were born. Sleep deprivation with a newborn baby is not a joke; it's an extreme mental and physical challenge. Somehow, I powered through this both times, successfully leading a nonprofit and then running my own business, but on occasion, I'll see something on the news that harkens back to 2011 or 2015—the years my daughters were born—and turn to my husband, saying, "I absolutely had no idea that celebrity so-and-so passed away or that X national event happened." Those weird moments of recounting the not-remembering wake me up as a manager that I should give the moms on my team extra support in the way of clarity around assignments. I venture to guess most moms will not be offended if you are ultra clear on what you need and by when; instead, they are likely to appreciate this additional support!

Take it from me as a mom and as a manager: if there is something important, especially a complex detail or a critical deadline, show grace and be direct in your communication with new moms by documenting what you need and by when so they are set up for success. Put it on all the team calendars, send an email in writing, and provide a nudge if needed. Those first months are fleeting in the grand scheme of your valued employee's time with you, and a boost of a reminder is a minimal amount of work for you and will go a long way toward creating success for you both. It is appreciated. This is an empathetic communication skill for managers of working moms.

Indirect Communication Can Signal Support, Too

While the thesis of this book is that you should have regular direct conversations with the working moms on your team, there are instances where indirect communications are appropriate and even helpful to bolster your efforts to support working moms. For example, put acknowledgments of success in writing for future performance reviews and so that when your working mom looks back in their fuzzy memory at this wild time of returning to work, they can visually see where you provided support and how they were succeeding.

Demonstrate your active listening by crafting team-building opportunities that reflect what working moms say they want and need. For example, every mom on my team expresses the same desire for stress relief: time and space away from child-rearing and away from task management at work, but with other adults for the comradery and even friendship that is so hard to find during the isolating years as a parent of young kids. With my team being fully remote, we have hosted various fun virtual experiences; we once had a Zoom meet-and-greet with an infamous reality-television celebrity that was just marvelous and hysterical. We have done paint-and-sip-type events to exercise our artistic muscles while chatting freely together. Another time, I set up a live online tour of a beekeeping sanctuary in Portugal over the lunch hour. It was a chance to drift off into another world for a bit, but alongside colleagues, which I know benefits my business by bonding team members and showing my commitment beyond the work in a way that they appreciate.

I am always sensitive about the timing of team building and events and either utilize a work lunch hour or poll my team to find an after-hours time past children's bedtimes. My goal is to support working moms and not create a situation where they end up having to catch up on work instead of having downtime at home because we took time out for team building. I also make sure—even if it takes us weeks to find a feasible date, given the variety of schedules my team keeps—to wait until we have a date and time that works for everyone so that the working mom who doesn't work on Fridays is not always left out. All these considerations are demonstrating through action my commitment to supporting working mothers on my team.

Consider acknowledging more than traditional measurements of success for the new moms on your team. Praise your team for skills that are freshly developed from this life transition. For example, I recently gave a shout-out in a group chat that one of my team members was incredibly impressive in her diplomacy. Sometimes my team engages with our social media followers on topics that can have more than one answer or involve some level of controversy, as a lot of parenting topics do. I made a point to praise that team member for more than just finishing the work on time or responding to X percent more customers that week; I told her how much I noticed that she was able to read the room and consider different perspectives. I can personally attest that these are skills learned by managing your own kids—which can be a full-time job of negotiating fights, handling toddler meltdowns when they don't get what they want, and navigating public spaces with little humans and their developing brains.

Finally, I often validate my team members with statements like *You really are a great mother* or *I can tell you work so hard at your parenting—it's impressive.* Especially when someone on my team is telling me about a situation with their kid that you can clearly tell they have been up nights worrying about, attending to, sacrificing for. I go out of my way to state the obvious: you are doing such a good job here at work and as a parent.

Measure the Effectiveness of Your Communication

This is a bit scary as a manager, boss, or supervisor—but I believe you should ask for feedback from your team, including your working moms, on your communication skills. Eek! I know. But here's the thing: If you are afraid of what they're going to say, you already know you need to change, right? In that case, the path forward is clear—training, learning, practicing.

Feedback makes us better, which is why we give it to our employees. The manager-communication evaluation questions could look something like this:

- Is there anything I could do to better communicate with you as a manager?
- Do you think my style of XYZ communication (e.g., weekly meeting, monthly call, task-management app) is clear and effective to help you complete your job objectives?

- Do you think we communicate often enough? Too often?
- Do you feel as though I hear you when we communicate? Do you feel validated and supported in our conversations?

The point of this exercise is not to ask the mom-support questions I will share with you in the next chapter; instead, it is to ensure your communication style resonates. This is going to help you be more efficient in your conversations with employees, more quickly be able to decode each employee's own style of communication, and again, by the nature of the questions, be able to reassure your working moms, and really all employees, that you truly care about them in your managerial communications.

Recognize That Each Employee Is Unique

By reaching out and asking the working moms on your teams what they want and need to feel supported and be successful at work, you will get at the heart of what is unique about the communication style of each member of your team. Like any group of employees, the moms you work with will have varying communication styles. This was confirmed in the surveys and interviews of working moms in my network: their comfort level with talking about their personal lives varied. However, the measurement of success in your communication with new moms is not the degree to which they spill information, but rather how valued and supported they feel in the workplace through your communications. For some working moms, you will create this goodwill with shorter, less specific conversations, and others will want to go deeper. The bottom line is as a Gallup study revealed: "Employees who feel as though their manager is invested in them as people are more likely to be engaged."[5] Engaged, valued, committed employees, including the moms on your team, are your objective as a manager and what is necessary for the success of your team.

In the above sections, I have outlined numerous ways you can set yourself on a track for best practices in your communication strategies and plan with working moms on your team. These strategies include the following:

1. Plan to engage.
2. Develop your questions.
3. Be ready to ask again—and again.
4. Develop and demonstrate empathy.
5. Choose timing wisely and aim for clarity.
6. Indirect communication can signal support, too.
7. Measure the effectiveness of your communication.
8. Recognize that each employee is unique.

---

5. Jim Harter and Amy Adkins, "What Great Managers Do to Engage Employees," *Harvard Business Review*, April 2, 2015, hbr.org/2015/04/what-great-managers-do-to-engage-employees.

A Note for Tired, Worried Managers

I wonder if by this point you might be a bit concerned as a manager of *all the things* and *all the people* that you do not have time, mental energy, or resources for. It is an absolutely fair and reasonable feeling; oh, the times I've been in bed at the end of a long day thinking, *Management is so, so draining.* I'm proposing a mindset shift: that you start thinking about support to working moms as an investment that will make your job *easier,* not harder. As mentioned earlier, this investment in communication and engagement can bail you out of detrimental cycles of hiring and rehiring people who do not stay because of lack of support. Or it can extinguish some of the fires you are having to constantly put out—performance issues, negative team morale, tensions. I am not proposing here that you take on any programs that you cannot afford or keep employees who are not the best fit for the organization; the goal of good communication with the moms on your teams, and the purpose of this book, is to help you polish and develop communication skills, empathy, and plans that support the working moms on your teams to perform at maximum happiness and success. The point is here is an up-front investment of time aimed at helping you and your entire team reach the organization's goals.

Speaking of your entire team, you might also be thinking, *How is this level of communication and support to working moms fair to everyone else on my team? Am I being asked here to give special treatment to working mothers?* I challenge you to throw away the notion of special treatment when it comes to working moms; special treatment to me is favoritism in choosing an employee for promotion who wasn't the lead candidate for the role, or clearly only making space and room for some members of your staff to speak in meetings or gain experience in new areas. Mothers have been a marginalized group at work since they entered the workforce; I think we're at low risk as a society of giving mothers special treatment. Nothing in this book suggests you should promote working mothers ahead of a better-qualified candidate or only care about their needs opposed to other employees' needs. Working moms have struggled to great detriment of their mental and physical health in the workplace and at home to achieve a healthy work–life balance and succeed in their careers. Providing them with the employer support they need to be successful in their job for your organization's success is not special treatment or favoritism.

Jumping off my soapbox, improving your support of working moms is about the development of management best practices and a healthy workplace culture. Strong communication skills and empathetic leadership styles are critical to managing everyone in the workplace, especially younger generations that expect you to care about them. The strategies you learn in this book and the efforts you make for working mothers are going to make a much happier team for everyone to work within. You can extend every bit of this support you learn here to each employee in their own unique way. Most people would like to be asked if they need support, to be checked on, to be appreciated, valued, and connected with. Being a manager who supports working moms is going to make you a great manager of *all* people.

6

The Manager's Road Map for Successful Conversations with Working Moms

B
y now you know that a conversation with new moms is a must-have. You've also been reminded of how valuable these employees are to your team and organization and that you don't want to see them go. You are awakened to the fact that working moms might be struggling a lot more than you previously realized, and you see that you need to be proactive in initiating an empathetic conversation about how you can better support them. But you may still not be clear on where to start. In this chapter, I will lay it all out for you: The topics you should consider broaching with new moms returning to work. Exactly how

to break the ice. When, where, and how to tackle any obstacles in conversation. To build your confidence and encourage you to start on this today, I'm going to share success stories of new moms and their managers talking about these issues so you can see that this simple solution *works*.

It's fine if a conversation is awkward; you try, and then you try again. Most moms are understanding when their bosses don't know exactly how to help; they just want to know that you *want* to help. I have felt this awkwardness myself as an employer: *What if talking about motherhood brings up hard emotions? What if they find breastfeeding too personal of a question for a manager to ask about? What if they ask for something I cannot deliver on or that is unfair to other employees?* Your conversations might knock it out of the park on the first try, or you might fumble a little, but when you take the initiative, you provide your working moms a chance to see your vulnerability, and you humanize the workplace for an employee in one of the most vulnerable periods of their life.

The first thing to consider is *how* to have these conversations. In most cases, that boils down to your work environment. But know this: moms tell me they can feel heard and supported in nearly every style of approach—in person, video conference, email, even text messages. It's ultimately about the good intention and seized opportunity. For instance, some moms reported receiving supportive text messages while out on leave from their bosses that made them feel much better about returning to the office. Other moms benefited from longer, more formal transition-planning meetings in-person. In the era of virtual and remote work, video conference and phone are acceptable modes of communication. It isn't so much about having the "perfect" conversation as having one at all—as well as follow-up conversations, too.

The conversation moms are wishing for, or lamenting the lack of, comes in several forms. It might literally be in the form of a question such as "How are you doing?" or "How can we support you?" One mom told me that the best conversations are framed as a powerful statement of support. Ann's boss, a manager in higher-education event planning, proactively came to her and said, "Tell me what you need, and we will figure out how to make it happen." Ann developed a deep loyalty to the manager and the organization. Her manager took the vulnerable position, not knowing what the mom would say in response—a leap of faith—and demonstrated a willingness to meet this mom wherever she was. Ann said she didn't ask for much in that first conversation, but it still left a lasting impression: *This organization cares about me. This is a place I want to work hard for.*

As you approach a conversation, keep in mind the potential new-mom anxiety and mental health challenges, the societal pressures to hide or downplay struggle, and the concerns about job stability and performance, and do what you can to create a safe space for a working mom to be honest with you. If you truly know what they need to be successful at work and can act on some or all of it, you have the key ingredients for a successful outcome.

Create a Transition Plan to Get Ahead of the Worry

Moms tell me that one of the most wished-for and proven successful tactics for a strong return to work is to have a transition plan in place before they even go out on leave. For some, the plan is formal and in writing, sometimes working from a template developed by human resources. For others, it's never called a "transition plan"; it's just a conversation that hits the same worry points and logistical concerns before the big motherhood event happens. Moms say that very early communication helps make the return to work more predictable and less daunting. It defuses a lot of unknowns, such as the following: *Will my boss support breastfeeding? How much flexibility will I really get with my schedule? Will I get approved to work from home part-time?* This can make a significant difference in a mom's enthusiasm to return to the job. Moms have shared with me that the best transition plans—or pregame pep talks—cover the following elements:

- Available benefits and resources for parents: insurance coverage for mental health services, how to get your child on insurance plans, support groups, tools for focus and organization

- Breastfeeding support: where and when to pump, lactation support, insurance coverage for a breast pump and supplies
- Scheduling opportunities and restrictions: flex time, modified scheduling, remote work for teams that don't always use it or never have
- Remote-work policies for teams already working this way: rules about camera on/off during meetings to protect breastfeeding privacy or for increased flexibility, childcare expectations for remote workers
- Ramp-up-after-leave opportunities: temporary part-time return, hybrid remote/in-person options, strategically starting back on a Wednesday instead of a Monday to lessen the first week stress
- Time off: Does a child being sick count as mom's sick time? What if you need to go over the allotted amount? Can you use vacation time for attending to family obligations?

Megan, an active-duty service member, told me how proactive her manager was in communicating about support before she had her baby. He clearly made an impact on her, and especially so because he did not share the working-mom experience, driving home the point that connection does not have to be made through fully understanding the situation but rather through empathy and good listening. Megan credited these conversations with a much smoother return to work:

When I reached the end of my first pregnancy, my boss approached me to ask if we could have a conversation to plan for how things would go for me when I returned from leave. I was so surprised that he had initiated this chat.

When we sat down, my boss asked, "What kind of schedule do you need for pumping?" and "Do you need help with a modified fitness and diet plan to support your postpartum period?" I hadn't even thought about these elements yet and was so appreciative he asked and helped me form a plan.

While I was on leave, I was comforted to know that the job plan was already in place and that I had a supervisor who was going to fully support me. It made my return to work 100 percent easier. When I came back, he reiterated his support and flexibility and made good on our plan.

Navigating all the stages of parenthood and how it interplays with work requires constant communication between employers and working parents. It's not a stagnant thing; it's constantly changing. Employers must take this into account and ensure the conversations and feedback are a recurring item. I'm lucky my boss was so attentive to this, and it has made a huge difference in my mental health and success on the job.

How do you initiate a conversation about a transition plan? Here are some helpful ways to open these conversations:

- How can we support you to get all the appropriate care you need during pregnancy?
- Is there anything here at work we could set up to make you comfortable during your pregnancy?
- What worries you the most about being out on leave?
- What worries you the most about your return to work coming back from leave?
- Would you like to know more about our support for breastfeeding moms?
- Would you like to work together on a transition plan for return to work?

If you miss the opportunity to create the plan before the mom goes on leave, don't think you've necessarily missed your only chance. Moms tell me they are happy to receive a communication toward the end of their leave from a boss asking how they can support them when they return. I recommend sending an email or text asking if the mom would like to talk about this while they are still on leave. Some moms might say no, but I think you'll find most will welcome the chance. Even if the mom has already returned to

173

work, moms tell me it is definitely not too late to ask how things are going and whether any plans or supports can be put in place to help. We're going to talk about exactly this in the next several sections, drilling down into some of the topics that should be in a transition plan.

Recognize that Your Plans or Moms' Plans Can Change

Now, we all know that "plans" sound a lot more set in stone than they usually are, especially when it comes to anything involving kids! The entire plan could change because a mom has an abrupt shift in her situation; pregnancy can suddenly have new obstacles like bed rest that require an earlier departure from the job. Becoming a parent often involves a major medical event, delivering a baby vaginally or by cesarean section, and there is no way to plan for how that is going to go. The baby could be born with needs not anticipated, or the mom might need to recover longer from birth complications. Parents may face a sudden change to an adoption timeline or need to take substantial time off to travel multiple trips for the process. Breastfeeding doesn't always come together as smoothly as might be hoped for. And, of course, in the weeks or months while a mom is out on maternity leave, the organization can change, too. But just as moms are often told by medical professionals to "have a birth plan but be open to things going a different way," so, too, do moms appreciate a back-to-work transition plan, understanding it is a work in progress that will evolve based on real-life experiences. You might need to take a different route in the end, but it's always good to create a map before you start.

You might consider putting the transition plan down on paper. Some elements will already be documented in your personnel or human resources policies, but others might emerge in conversation. If you're not comfortable writing them down, that's fine, but capturing the conversation in a summary email after the meeting ensures everyone involved heard the same thing—also allowing you to copy the email to any other stakeholders, such as additional supervisors or human resources—and it will remind you months later when your working mom returns (operating on extremely limited sleep) about exactly what you discussed. Transition plans do not have to be complicated. Here's a sample email from manager to working mom sharing a transition plan:

To: Working Mom

From: Manager

Subject: Congratulations & Follow-Up

It was great meeting with you today about your exciting news. Congratulations again on your pregnancy! We're all really excited for you. Per our conversation, here are the key points we discussed today as a starting point:

- Please reference the Employee Handbook for the maternity-leave policy. We also agreed that you would confirm with human resources some of your technical questions about paid leave. Please report back to me what you hear so that we are all clear and I can make sure it goes smoothly for you.
- You indicated your goal to use a breast pump at work, and I provided you with your rights under the law for breastfeeding breaks. I'd also strongly encourage you to talk to [Other Working Mom] in our office, who is currently pumping, as she's offered to provide some great tips and resources for scheduling time in the lactation room. If there is anything else you need for successful pumping here at work, please let me know.
- You indicated you need flexibility now and after the baby is born for doctor's appointments, and we agreed that you can take flex time as needed. Let's keep a conversation going about this topic as your needs at work evolve.
- You mentioned concern about balancing work and life after you return, and I am attaching a resource that we provide for employees. We cover therapy telehealth, offer an online course about returning to work after becoming a parent, and even host a weekly lunch-bunch support group for families.

I'm also open to reviewing any other ideas you might have—please send them my way.

I know you're just getting started thinking about this big life transition; I wanted you to know you have our full support and my door is open anytime you want to talk about what you need. I'll also be touching base with you by text before the end of your leave, if that's okay with you, to see if there is anything we can do to best prepare for your return, and we'll meet again in person after you return. We truly value you here at this organization and look forward to being a part of your parenting journey. You got this!

Communicate Clearly About Benefits, Policies, and Laws (Don't Just Refer Everyone to HR)

Moms say that one of the most critical functions of the manager–mom conversation is explaining the benefits, organizational policies, and applicable laws that relate to the new-mom experience, whether there is a human resources department or not. Many first-time moms are overwhelmed physically and mentally with this massive life change and haven't really absorbed the latest happenings on legal protections for breastfeeding or the Family and Medical Leave Act (FMLA). They may not understand the extent to which their organization offers flexibility in scheduling, sick time, and so on. They may have an incorrect understanding of benefits or policies as relayed to them from other staff. This is a basic conversation that needs to happen right off the bat, a crash course on all they need to know in their new realm. Many will be tapping into aspects of their benefits policies they hadn't thought much about before, and it's possible that policies have changed since the last time they looked at the employee handbook. The moms I spoke with for this book also shared that a manager clearly understanding the benefits of the organization and the policies and laws for working parents is an indication of their investment in their employees' well-being.

This conversation is bigger and broader than your leave policy and ideally happens way before the mom goes on leave. Most moms tell me they want to have this conversation soon after announcing they are going to become parents, particularly about their leave since that requires extensive planning, financially and logistically, for their job roles. To the extent you are allowed to share about any forthcoming changes to benefits, policies, or flexibility, they want that information with as much advance notice as possible. For instance, if you expect that remote work will be an option by the time they have a baby, they would love to talk about utilizing that benefit; conversely, if remote work is offered now and you see that phasing out, that, too, would be important for these moms to know so there are no surprises. Ideally, working moms would like to have the opportunity to contribute ideas and feedback about the policies and benefits that impact their families.

Erin, the admin from chapter one who had high praise for her organization's compassionate leadership, shared an interesting story about how strong communication with her managers made all the difference in her working-mom experience:

When I announced I was pregnant, I first told my human resources director, who is my immediate supervisor. Work is such a major part of my life that I told work before my own mom! It was important for me to tell my director because I really didn't know how to navigate this for the first time; I had no idea what the benefits were or what resources might be available.

My boss asked if I had signed up for short-term disability, and thankfully, I had known about that and had signed up. She then looked up all the current benefits available to me, like the Family and Medical Leave Act, what is and is not covered under sick leave, [and] how the short-term disability would work, and explained our paid-time-off program. I was amazed. She gave me a thorough review of everything available to me in the first two or three months of my pregnancy before I had even shared the good news with everyone else. This was so reassuring.

Because the news of my pregnancy was so supported by my boss, I shared it with our CEO early on, too. She was so awesome in explaining how the company could be supportive. Then, later on when I had a little bit of an awkward encounter, it was no big deal because the conversations had become regular and comfortable.

I'll be honest with you. As I got physically larger in my pregnancy and increasingly uncomfortable, I got lax in my professional attire. I had moved away from the corporate office shirts or dresses I had once worn and was now wearing large sweatpants or leggings. The CEO came to me one day and suggested that I invest in just a couple of pieces of maternity clothing that would be both comfortable for me and more presentable in the office, fitting their policy for customer-client expectations. They brought this uncomfortable topic to me with such compassion and acknowledgment for why I would be feeling physically uncomfortable, and because we previously had so many great conversations about support, I didn't feel offended. It was really a good reminder about how I want to present myself to clients while still wanting to be comfortable.

When you tell your boss that you are pregnant, there is so much fear about job loss and instability, and anxiety that everyone will think your pregnancy and new parenthood is a hindrance to your productivity. I felt the opposite. I felt empowered by my bosses and appreciated because the leadership immediately made me feel important and clear about how things would go for me. They were there for me every step of the way. They even gave me some helpful advice on professional maternity fashion when I didn't know what I was doing!

Here are some great conversation starters:

- What questions do you have about our organization's policies and benefits for families?
- Let's schedule a meeting to review benefits and policies that relate to parenting so we can both learn what's available to you.
- Did you know that we have XYZ benefit that you could take advantage of as a new parent?
- Would you like to hear more about the supports we have for breastfeeding moms?
- What kind of information or resources can we provide to you to make you more comfortable or support you during your pregnancy?

One of the great things about offering information is that it helps you assess whether a mom is struggling in this area or wants your support without putting her in an uncomfortable position. For instance, *Would you like to hear more about the benefits we have for postpartum mental health support?*—which might be a few sessions of teletherapy that your organization covers—would send a signal to the working mom: *We care about your mental health. It's safe to talk about this topic here.* Benefits and policy discussion can feel a bit boring or formal, but they also can break the ice for a conversation about a whole host of important topics your working moms might want and need to talk about.

Be Ready in Interviews

I discussed earlier in the book that some women are feeling more empowered to ask prospective employers about working-mom support, whether they are a mom yet or not. Based on our understanding of millennial and Gen Z parents, who have a higher expectation of flexible and supporting workplaces, this is an area you will want to be prepared for in the years to come. While earlier I reminded you of the types of biased, judgmental, and possibly illegal questions that should not be asked of candidates or employees, you should be ready to answer questions about support. Certainly, the starting point is to know your benefits and policies for families inside and out, but there is more to consider as you enter the hiring process. Here are some examples of things to bring up in your interviews:

- What kinds of family support are you interested in hearing about so I can tailor our conversation to your interests?
- Would you be interested in talking with a member of my staff about our workplace culture? I am happy to connect you with someone. (I recognize this is not possible in all confidential hiring processes, but I know I did this often in smaller organizations when I had already made an offer and my candidate was still deciding.)
- We review our supports for families on an annual basis. Last year, our team had some really great suggestions, and we implemented the following: X event, Y new benefit.
- I maintain an open-door policy and regularly schedule meetings and coffee chats with my team to make sure that all team members feel supported on topics of mental health, work–life balance, and family priorities. I would welcome you to take advantage of these.
- Would you like a tour of our lactation room before you leave? I could show you our events calendar coming up for team building and give you the website of our family-resource group.

Get Comfortable Talking About
Breastfeeding at Work

This is a hot, hot topic for many working moms because it's one of the most distinctly different things you might do at work as a new mom that you didn't do at work before, and thus, it requires some planning and change to the usual work rhythm. What goes into planning for this or how to navigate it once back at the job can be a huge mystery to many first-time moms, and certainly might be to employers. Pumping in person at a job, or even remotely for that matter, brings a multitude of logistical, scheduling, and financial challenges. If you add in additional factors like being in a job that has field work and travel—just ask moms who pump in their patrol car, hotel conference room, or airport lounge—it can be a challenge to navigate working and pumping.

It's impossible for working moms to predict how the breastfeeding journey will go for them or exactly how it will feel or work out to pump on the job. They may have guidance and support from lactation providers or their friends or family about pumping at work, but it's truly one of those you-don't-know-what-it's-like-until-you-do-it situations. More than 80 percent of American moms initiate breastfeeding, and 60 percent are still going when their baby is six months old, likely well after they are back on the job with you—in other words, breastfeeding is a significant and meaningful topic for managers to address with working mothers.[1]

Not only are we obligated to give working moms our attention on the topic of breastfeeding, but also, they truly want our support on this topic. Working moms want managers to understand that, for many moms, breastfeeding is a crucial part of their parenting beliefs and goals, and that once they start down the path of breastfeeding, it's medically necessary to pump on a routine basis or risk getting an infection or experience a decline in breast milk supply. I have many amazing examples of managers navigating breastfeeding at work. Here's one from Olivia, a nurse:

> *I've had two different but great experiences with my managers proactively supporting my breastfeeding goals. After having my first child, my boss, without prompting from me, stated the location of the mother's room and made it clear: we will accommodate your breastfeeding needs. This was at a very small company with a lot of new moms, and they clearly knew the ropes of what moms wanted and needed; they even provided me with a calendar for use of the room so we could schedule time so as not to overlap.*

---

1. "Key Breastfeeding Indicators," Centers for Disease Control and Prevention, accessed October 20, 2021, www.cdc.gov/breastfeeding/data/facts.html.

When I had my second baby, I worked at our local hospital in a much larger system. Not only did my boss offer me a private room to pump, but they even provided the pump equipment! They also handed me lactation-support information and let me set my own schedule.

I've had such wonderful accommodations from management and supportive coworkers. I still have friendships with the mothers I met while on the pumping schedule, too, which has helped me create a community of family throughout different parts of my job.

Working moms also say that it is possible for managers to talk with moms about breastfeeding and show support without personally understanding the experience. Carly, a marine biologist, told me:

I met with my boss and told them I was pregnant. This is an exciting and frightening thing to do. My boss immediately asked, "How can I support you when you return after the birth of your baby?" From there, we worked together on ideas. For example, I told my boss that breast pumping was important to me and that it isn't really feasible to do it physically outside in the field. The boss didn't know a lot about breastfeeding, but we just talked it out. And our brainstorming session resulted in my boss saying they would swap duties with me so that I would handle the inside responsibilities, and they would take the outside responsibilities so that I could have a smoother transition in and out of my pump sessions.

From this first conversation, I've felt that my boss has worked to get me exactly what I needed, including the accommodation of a place to pump, and this makes me feel appreciated and happy to be at work.

In addition to cheering on your breastfeeding employees and providing useful information about the law or location of a lactation room, you can be proactive on logistics. Moms frequently tell me the best experiences with managers are when the manager sees a logjam in the system and takes action to help the team. Keep your eyes and ears open to how you might intervene to make a difference for these moms. Below are two examples of how managers successfully fixed problems they saw for breastfeeding moms. Nicole, a home-lending underwriter, said:

I was sitting at my desk about a week after I came back from maternity leave. I was just about to finish my lunch break. I get an hour for lunch, but I had only been taking thirty minutes so I could eat and pump and then use another thirty minutes later in the afternoon to use the breast pump again.

My boss came in that day and said, "You are not doing anything wrong, but you are entitled to have your full lunch hour and an extra break apart from lunch for breastfeeding." I was so blown away by this generous observation. She said, "We want you to have a good lunch and meet your pumping needs; both are important to your functionality on the job."

Wow, I cannot even tell you how much I felt supported. My company was looking out for me, even if it meant a little more time off the clock. I was really impressed they took the initiative to reach out to me about this. I hadn't realized that I wasn't using the time that they were giving me.

Alejandra, an Amazon fulfillment-center associate, benefited from a boss who intervened to make the pumping experience more efficient for everyone:

All it took was some creativity by one of my bosses to support breastfeeding at our fulfillment center. All of us associates have the same lunch break. Because it's a new facility, there is just one mother's room so far as they are still building out the site, and several moms [need] to pump. This makes it hard to go and use the pumping room, because anyone needing to pump was there at the same time and there wasn't space.

My manager took it upon herself to bring up the issue to upper management. They worked together to create a sign-up sheet for thirty-minute pumping-room time slots so we don't overlap with each other.

*All of us pumping moms benefited by this man-
ager who advocated for us to get the logistical support
we need to pump. It's better for everyone: we're able
to pump, and there isn't a backlog of people waiting
around or struggling to figure out when they can go
pump. It made us all feel supported, like they were
working with us to figure out the problem, not leaving
us to struggle on our own.*

Showing your support for working moms' breastfeeding goals is a key part of creating a workplace where moms
feel understood. That does not mean you have to know
what it feels like or have experienced breastfeeding to provide empathy to a mom in the throes of her journey. It just
means you make sure the pieces are in place for a successful
experience and speak up when you see roadblocks tripping
up your employees.

Bring the Whole Team on the Same Page

My focus thus far has been on your direct conversations
with working moms, the topics and issues that concern
them, and removing obstacles to their success as a parent
and as your employee. There is also some homework for you
during the in-between times: when your working mom is
on leave or between the chats or meetings you have. This is
the time to build support with the rest of the team.

In larger organizations, educating colleagues and other employees may involve human resources in the conversation. In any size organization, rallying everyone to support working moms includes creating and modeling a culture of support beyond manager/mom. Here's an example of what I mean by this. If you tell a mom that you support their breast-feeding goals, then show them the lactation space, brief them on the coverage for a breast pump through the organization's insurance plan, and point out that they can take the time to pump. Make sure the rest of the team understands and respects this plan. In chapter one, we talked about the struggles some moms face with coworkers. Uninformed or resentful coworkers can undermine all your hard work in this area. So as your working mom nears their return-to-the-job date, loop in coworkers. Explain to your other team members how valuable the moms are to your team or organization and how excited you are for the employee's return from leave, and remind employees of the company policies and to demonstrate empathy for the new challenges they'll face. Make sure your well-formed plans can play out successfully in practice.

To build team support for working mothers, issues of transition for working mothers need to be regularly out in the open in conversation. For example, you might consider dedicating time at a staff meeting to cover key benefits and expectations for supporting families. Make the case that supporting working moms is better for the organization using some of the key points I shared in chapter two. You can create a culture of support in your organization that ultimately helps all generations, such as flexible schedules and leave that supports situations beyond parental leave, including leave to care for an elderly parent or to help a sick partner and so forth. A sample memo to the team—that would also serve as talking points for an in-person or Zoom in-service—could include something like this:

MEMO

To: X Company Department of Y

From: The Manager

Re: Supporting Families Creates Success

One of the core values at our organization is supporting families. There have been a lot of great changes and evolutions at our company in terms of new mom support the last few years that I wanted to be sure you are aware of.

- Breastfeeding support: Under the new federal law, breastfeeding employees are provided a space and protected break time to use their breast pump. We want our breastfeeding employees to feel empowered; we've also added a mini fridge to the pump space to help streamline milk storage. You might not relate to this experience, but we should still support it.

- Parental leave: We are proud to offer a robust parental-leave option for both mothers and fathers and believe that this is an important time for families to focus on their family.
- Flexible scheduling: Families can take advantage of our shared paid-time-off program with other team members and utilize remote work as approved by their supervisor(s); while we have high expectations for performance, we also believe family is a top priority.
- Mental health support: Especially after the challenging last few years for us all, mental health is a top priority for everyone on the team, including me. We have robust mental health supports such as telehealth sessions available for all employees, including new parents. I also encourage you to speak with me anytime you are feeling like you need support, whether you are a parent or not.

All our employees are valuable and critical to the success of the organization, including those with young children, and it takes our entire team's effort to create a culture where we support working families. My door is open to help you understand policies and laws for working families, to discuss any concerns, and to make continual improvements to our work culture. Join me in making this a truly family-friendly environment—and a workplace our whole team can be proud of!

You can take this support even further. Consider starting a working group, task force, or informal meetup for working families and present on these topics to the whole team at a lunch, retreat, or staff meeting. Share stories. Have working mothers share how company benefits have made all the difference in their experience at the job or offer ways in which colleagues can support their personal growth during this transitional time. Forward your team's meaningful developments in support for families—for instance, send updates on legislative policy changes in support of families. The most successful way to build colleague support for working mothers is to get the rest of the team invested and bought in to the value, and *joy*, of supporting working mothers. They will see and feel the results of a positive workplace, and the working mothers on your team will want to stay.

Identify All the Challenges and Partner for All the Solutions

As you have learned through these chapters, there are many possible challenges for each working mom and organization. One mom might identify postpartum depression as a struggle, while another needs support on scheduling flexibility. The need might be breastfeeding support or help finding adequate childcare options. Working with each individual mom on what they want and need is how you get to the heart of the issues and create solutions as a manager. Allison, a retail manager, shared an example of manager-mom success:

> I accept that working in retail management nights, weekends, and most holidays is a requirement of the job. But even though the job demands this, my manager still makes me feel heard and that my needs are important.
>
> When I announced I was pregnant with my second child, my manager immediately told me: "If you have any appointments you need to attend, or when baby comes and you need time for those appointments, please do not hesitate to communicate to me, and we'll work around it."
>
> Then, after I had my baby, whenever the store managers make our monthly schedule, they always make sure I'm okay with the schedule before it is finalized so that I can work around my son's needs.
>
> These small conversations where they ask me about my schedule and make me feel like parenting is taken seriously have made me feel so supported from pregnancy all the way through to being a new mom.

Here are some additional questions you might integrate into your conversations with working moms:

- What kinds of tools and resources could we provide to support you as a new mom?
- What kinds of tools and resources could we provide to support you in your job?
- How we can best support you now that you're back from leave?
- How is your baby sleeping and doing? How are *you* feeling as a new mom? How are things going for you?
- Is there anything that worries you about balancing work and motherhood that we could help you with?
- How is the work schedule panning out for you?
- How are the childcare options that are available to you?

Remember Patricia, the mom whose story I shared in the discussion about mental health in chapter one? She suffered in silence until the day it all came crashing down, very publicly, at work. While the manager–mom communication should have come before the breaking point, it really is never too late to support a working mom. In Patricia's case, the crisis became an organizational catalyst for a better workplace. I am excited to share more of her story with you here:

On paper, before my mental health struggles were out in the open, I was a great employee since I met deadlines and went above and beyond the tasks asked of me. I was always passed over for promotions, though, and I think it's because I never stood out from the crowd—clearly, work experience alone wasn't cutting it. I thought managers must not have crazy personal lives like mine, and I've got to keep mine under wraps if I want respect at work.

After that incident at the office, I began therapy for postpartum anxiety/postpartum depression, which not only gave me tools to manage my mental health but also led to incredible personal growth. Without professional help, I never would have been able to turn my feelings of anxiety, despair, and fragmentation into growth. Also, I learned after the fact that my therapy is covered by my employer-provided insurance, which I'm extremely grateful for since I'd never have been able to afford it on my own.

Being vulnerable about my mental health—and ultimately, my managers taking note and getting involved—allowed everyone to see me as a whole person, flaws and strengths. I think that's critical for success in any environment. My managers also saw my willingness to seek help and grow. And guess what—I got a promotion!

The honesty and transparency and conversations that came out of this situation were not off-putting as I had feared, but instead created a better relationship *with my manager, which landed me a new role and gave me the courage to start up a working-parents group to help others out in the same situation before there is a crisis next time.*

It is empowering to know we have that much control and impact on our teams in such simple ways. It isn't only a matter of policies and benefits; we hold a key right in our hands through our management style.

To recap, here are the ways in which I've laid out a road map for your conversations with working moms:

1. Create a transition plan to get ahead of the worry.
2. Recognize that your plans or moms' plans can change.
3. Communicate clearly about benefits, policies, and laws (don't just refer everyone to HR).
4. Be ready in interviews.
5. Get comfortable talking about breastfeeding at work.
6. Bring the whole team on to the same page.
7. Identify all the challenges and partner up for all the solutions.

Imagine how much of an impact you could make as a manager through having conversations, sharing resources, and creating a culture of support for working moms. Your efforts will pay off for your team's and organization's success.

7

Sustainable Support for Working Moms

I n this book, I have pinpointed the critical supports working moms need and want, as shared with me over the past decade by moms across sectors and in organizations big and small. I have shared the unique and valuable skill sets many working moms bring to our sales podiums, factory floors, and conference tables, as evidenced in consumer surveys, organizational performance statistics, and the stories I have shared. I have laid out the business case for how working moms are important to recruit and retain because they are additive to your organization's bottom line, and I have shown that providing support to working moms saves your organization money. I have cited research that proves that future women leaders need strong manager support to navigate career advancement and personal family growth. I have exposed the barriers for working moms to speak up and ask for help from their managers and have reflected on why initiating communication with working moms could be hard for managers as well. I have highlighted proactive communication as *the most* important tool for manager and team success, and I have shared stories of moms who have struggled or succeeded in their return to work and what they say they need from their managers.

Where we land now at the end of this book is the jumping-off point for you to get going on these critical con- versations with the working mothers on your team. In these final pages, I will share stories to illustrate the most efficient and effective work environment for working moms, where managers can lead productive and satisfied teams for the best possible organizational outcomes. Through the inten- tional efforts of bosses, managers, supervisors, and leaders, these are the teams where support is so ingrained in the culture of the organization that moms speak up for what they need and when they need it, which creates sustainable support in your workplace. I mentioned earlier in the book that there are many resources out there aimed at working moms on how to advocate for what they need to be suc- cessful on the job; it is my firm belief that the key to being a successful advocate for yourself is to have a manager who creates an environment where the mom can be fully heard with their needs met. By this point, you understand that asking moms what they need is the starting point for all aspects of creating support; where you take it to the next level is by creating a sustainable culture of support where all your employees, including working moms, *come to you* when they need help.

Support Can Happen Anywhere

Payton, a mom who I had the pleasure of corresponding with for months while writing this book, works on the factory floor of a Fortune 500 heavy-equipment manufacturing company. Her job in a male-dominated industry is not really where a lot of us would expect to find a model for management support of working moms. Payton's company does have large financial resources to provide employees with benefits and programs. They have a robust human resources department, and some of their workers are unionized. But at the same time, the bureaucracy of running an international company with dozens and dozens of locations, steeped in heavily negotiated employee pay and benefits policies, and operating in an industry that could easily be attached to old ways of leading teams, creates a unique and interesting story to tell. What we will learn from Payton's experience is that managers can support working moms in meaningful ways in all sorts of organizations, big or small; corporate, nonprofit, or small business; back office or factory floor; one-office location or across many locations;

union or nonunion; and irrespective of a manager's parent status or gender and, frankly, whether higher leadership cares or not. We will also see that when managers make the investment in creating a supportive environment, the culture perpetuates itself. This investment not only helps working moms—and other employees—thrive; it also eases the load on managers.

Payton's manager invests time in building up people in a way that promotes their success and potential, while also creating a safe space for employees to ask for what they need. Payton shared with me:

> *The support the company provides attracts women who want jobs and a family to the company. We are known for being family friendly and supportive. It would take a lot for me to leave this company. The culture and benefits far surpass competitors. But most of all, the support my manager has provided me has made it impossible to imagine working for any other company that does not support me and my family's needs at this level. For me, family comes first, and the job is secondary. If I cannot be there physically, emotionally, and mentally for my family, the job is not worth it. The company, and my manager, acknowledge this and demonstrate that they get it. I cannot wait to tell you more.*

As Payton's story unfolded inside my inbox, I realized that her manager's approach travels the pathway I've discussed throughout this book. Specifically, Payton's manager does the following:

1. Initiates conversations to find out what support working moms want and need, then acts by connecting employees to existing resources or develops new resources, flexibilities, or solutions.
2. Demonstrates empathy and creates connections that spur a feeling of trust and safety between manager and employees, whether or not he has a personal experience with the topic.
3. Enlists other people and resources to provide working moms with additional help, which enhances the support and takes a burden off of the manager.
4. Creates an environment where working moms speak up freely when they need help, have ideas for better support, or face challenges coming back to the job.

As you will read below, Payton's manager ended up creating a sustainable culture of support for working mothers. He continues to nurture the relationships and set new moms on the path to support as they come back to the factory floor; the intentional conversations, empathy shown, and connections to other resources have created a place where Payton and other moms can advocate for themselves without hesitation, which is truly the end goal here.

Payton's Manager Initiates the Conversations

Proactive conversations with working moms really stick; they make a positive impression and go a long way to creating the kind of workplace where your team will fully apply their efforts and stick around for a long time. Payton's manager jumped in right from the start to take the initiative to ask important questions that made her feel heard, seen, and valued:

My boss asks what I need to be successful as a working mother. One time, we had this short conversation that had a huge impact on me. I needed to use a breast pump back on the factory floor. I was thinking about it and wondering how I was going to navigate it. He asked if I would need that [pumping] support. When I said I did, he told me to turn off the radio when it was time to pump, don't worry about my union breaks, and he said, "Take the time you need—feeding your child comes first." I cannot even begin to tell you how surprised and delighted I was.

In addition to the direct conversations prompted by her manager, the company where Payton works goes above and beyond in supporting breastfeeding employees. Leadership and human resources also thoroughly train their managers to know what the benefits and accommodations are, how to use them, and how to communicate about them. Payton shared with me some of the components of this robust lactation support that she receives from her company:

> *Each factory or office location for my company has a new mother's—or wellness—room. These rooms have a chair, sink, and refrigerator, which I know is more than a lot of moms get in other companies. Some have freezers as well, which is such a nice recognition by management that we need to store the milk according to health guidelines. At some locations, they stock extra "goodies" like breast pads or milk-storage bags. It makes you feel so good that they provide those little items that you know are nice to have and not must-have. You can feel the support.*
>
> *Each room has a lock for privacy and several locations require a key or passcode to get in. They care not just about having a nice space for us but also creating a good system. For instance, each room has a calendar so that it can be booked like a conference room so there are not conflicts between employees. This is also extremely helpful if visiting another location and you do not know the schedule of colleagues working at that space all the time! You could tell that management*

was thinking ahead and getting feedback—avoiding scheduling conflicts, making transition between work locations seamless and efficient, considering health and safety, and going above and beyond to create a feeling of support for new moms.

At this point in my conversation with Payton, I could tell she really feels the support, and then she shared how her manager and company leadership have taken the breast-feeding support to yet another level:

The company pays to ship breast milk home when a mom is traveling for work. This was huge for me when I had to be away from my new baby for work. This is something all companies should provide for moms who must travel for work. It made the logistics of breastfeeding away from home easier, and I felt like the company understood how important breastfeeding is to me, and that I'm a mother even on the road, by offering this.

Payton's manager and company did not wait around for federal policies to dictate how to provide support; they talked with their working-mom employees to learn what the pain points were in navigating the workplace while balancing parenthood, and they put in place solutions.

The support Payton has found from her manager and company extend far beyond lactation support; we also discussed at length how mental health is one of the top areas of support working moms asked for in her company. Managers learned what support their employees need and sent those requests—in this case, mental health services—up the chain of command, resulting in companywide benefits. Payton shared with me the kind of benefits that resulted from what employees said they want and need:

> When it comes to mental health, the bosses aren't just saying they support you; they show you they mean it in the resources made available. Specifically, my company provides counseling sessions for each mental health "event" you experience so that you are not having to figure out which issue is the worse one or most important to deal with—you can address it all. For example, I can get five free sessions for having a life change, like having a baby. Then I could have five more sessions to talk about postpartum anxiety or depression as a new diagnosis or topic. This is a support that helps a lot of employees, and I love that we can use it for each challenge we face. It does not feel limited or just for the company to look good on paper.

After talking with Payton, I researched her company a bit more deeply, curious to know more about the demographics of workers and leadership. Her company is comprised of just 30 percent women, and therefore it is not likely that moms dominate the place. But they have robust working-mom supports! You need not be a working mom to support working moms. Savvy managers and company leadership who have listened to the issues brought to them by their empowered employees aim to be two steps ahead of support needs.

Payton's Manager Demonstrates Empathy

When I surveyed working moms in my network, 89 percent said that if they had a boss who connected with them on personal topics at work, they would feel more comfortable bringing their own challenges to the table for help. When an opportunity presents itself to toss out a personal tidbit that would make you more relatable as a manager, it is worth doing. You might just get information back from the working moms on your teams that will shake loose some strategies to improve the workplace and performance or explain an obvious tension or issue you have been observing. Payton's manager reaches his employees by building connections and showing empathy:

> *My manager shares about his family and some of the struggles they have faced as they relate to what his employees are going through. It makes it easier to share about my own challenges. It's nice to see the person behind the professional, so to speak. Even if the issues we both face aren't related. Knowing that others*

have their own struggles helps us to see the humanity in them. It also helps getting to know the person and what they like to do outside of work.

Just last week, my kiddo threw up at daycare, and I had to leave work to get him. My team covered for me, and I never felt that I made the wrong decision or that I left people hanging at work. I have covered for others in similar situations, including my manager, who needed support! It feels great that our whole team can be there for each other, and it's logistically helpful for work. I absolutely recommend managers getting to know their employees personally. I hope I can be that kind of manager when I get the chance.

Imagine what it would be like to have team members who feel so understood that they have *your* back in a time of need. Imagine having employees who are so self-sufficient in initiating what they need to be successful that they identify solutions and get you that information so you can act quickly and without a lot of added stress on you as manager.

Payton's Manager Enlists Help in Supporting Moms

Being in management is stressful, and there are many days where managers feel they do not have the bandwidth to provide significant support to employees. Ironically, I often feel some of the same feelings of fatigue in parenting as I do in management—I just cannot tackle one more emotion, need, task, or conversation. And if you start down this path in a workplace where support hasn't been part of the culture, there may be some heavy lifting to get things going—I went through the many ways you can kickstart these support conversations in chapter six. There are many ways in which a manager can get help in providing support. Here's an example from Payton:

> *The company set up a new moms' group! My manager connected me to this group when I needed support. This is a collection of parents passionate about sharing their motherhood experiences. There are monthly talks about different topics such as childcare, family leave, and so on. They provide question sheets for childcare, mentoring resources, maternity-leave planning documents, and guides for managers. We also have an online chat to ask questions in between meetings. This has been one of the absolute best resources at work. It gives me a lot of places and ways to get support.*

Once the manager got the ball rolling, he connected Payton and her colleagues to other resources that could keep the momentum going. This support also gives Payton's manager a break from having to shoulder the full load of responsibility.

Payton's Manager's Efforts Have Become Sustainable

Nearly three-quarters of the working moms in my network said that the ideal working environment is one where the boss asks questions *and* moms feel safe to bring up issues on their own. These moms accept that they, too, have the responsibility to speak. However, they also said they need their managers to send signals that it is okay to share and that they won't face any kind of serious employment risk or cultural retaliation. In fact, only 25 percent of the moms said that they work in an environment where they are comfortable, without hesitation, to speak up about personal issues with their managers. Think about that for a moment—*three-quarters of the working moms I surveyed said that they do not feel comfortable speaking up*, or if they do, they anticipate having negative consequences at work. That is a stunning amount of discomfort in the workplace. Even if you think you have created a supportive workplace for your team, it is worth evaluating to be certain—I'll tell you how to go about evaluating this in the next section. When I asked Payton about the idea of advocating on her own behalf, she said this:

> *Having my manager's support makes speaking up much less sticky and confrontational. Working for a company that values people and follows antidiscrimination laws has been a huge benefit in my favor for my approach. My manager has always demonstrated*

a commitment to creating a family-friendly culture, which really helps me feel comfortable and safe in asking for what I need. I have never felt like my family should not be the most important thing in my life. Without this kind of support from my company and manager, I would absolutely leave the job.

Not only do most working moms in my surveys feel uncomfortable speaking up, but over 50 percent said it is a deal-breaker to stay in a job long-term where they don't feel okay asking for what they need. This leaves us managers and organizations on the brink of losing some of our most valued team members.

Managers Are the Changemakers

After talking with Payton extensively about her experience with her manager, I imagined what it would be like to be in her shoes, working in that job under that manager. This is what I imagined I would "hear" if I were Payton, stringing together all these robust benefits, supports, and responsive policies during this big life transition:

Payton, welcome back from your sixteen-week paid maternity leave! Before you left, we had multiple transition-planning conversations and connected you with all the resources available so you feel comfortable and eager to return. Now that you are back, do you plan to breastfeed? Yes? We fully support that and believe it is a priority. We have time and space for lactation. And refrigerators specifically for milk. At every jobsite location. And if we ask you to travel away from home, we will ship your milk back home to baby. And if you have questions about how to make it all work, we'll hook you up with Human Resources.

We also have an employee resource group, the new moms' group, which can also support you and answer your questions. If your child is sick, your colleagues and your manager will have your back and help cover your work. And if you find yourself experiencing mental health struggles along the way, we have support for that, too. Each time you need it. For more than one session. There's no expiration to this support! As your manager, I can absolutely relate to these big life transitions, and my door is always open to discuss any support you need. I'll also follow up with you in the months to come to see how I can help. And I hope that you will always feel comfortable coming to me with anything you might need.

I want to work there and stay in that job, don't you? It can be done in any industry. Even when 70 percent of the employees and 60 percent of the management are men who have not had the new-mom experience, as is the case where Payton works. Even if the kind of resources that Payton's company offers are outside the scope of your operational budget. You as a manager can compensate with communication, flexibility, empathy, showing vulnerability, and getting creative, even when your company cannot afford to ship breast milk overnight.

Realistically, even in a company with great benefits on paper and great managers in some departments, not all working-mom employees have a positive experience. I looked up Payton's company on a couple of job-review websites. Generally, the company receives strong marks on work–life balance compared to their competitors. I did read some one-star reviews about a pressured work environment and demanding hours unsuitable for a healthy personal life in certain departments. I want to acknowledge that I saw these comments, even though I am loving everything about Payton's supportive experience, because, especially at larger companies, it all comes back to—you guessed it—*managers*. Payton spoke about this when she shared the following with me:

Support of families, children, and family situations in my company is dependent on the manager and team. Each team has its own culture, and many are very supportive of taking time as needed for kiddos—regardless of whether you are Mom or Dad. For all teams I have been a part of, family has come first and leaving for child/family needs is never a concern.

Organization culture, policies, and employee benefits are critical tools that empower managers to help make working-mom support truly exceptional, but managers themselves make it or break it for their employees. Payton's manager has taken the strong company benefits and policies and harnessed them to make the working moms on his team feel supported. Another manager could just as easily lack awareness of these supports, neglect to share them, or even create barriers to accessing the benefits. We heard examples like that in many of the challenging stories earlier in the book, like the critical care nurse whose employer provided a lactation room that she could not reach in the allotted time for breastfeeding, creating a functional problem to utilizing support benefits. Or the mom who worked in a bank where work and childcare end at the same time but are not in the same building, creating an unworkable scheduling situation. Or the mom who was so overwhelmed on her first day back to work finding every hour on her calendar scheduled in a way that she could not catch her breath to ask for the help and guidance she needed.

Support comes down to managers. Here's a telling example from Madison, a transportation engineer who works in a company where leadership is entirely unsupportive of working moms, but whose manager still makes her experience supportive. She shared with me:

When COVID-19 hit, we were sent home in March 2020, then we were brought back in the office in May 2020 because leadership wanted us back in. I was really worried, and the leadership of the company was insensitive to the reality for working moms at that time. Most of the daycares had not reopened, we were afraid of getting sick and bringing that home to our kid, our partners were not working in person yet, school wasn't in person, and there were so many other unknowns. My son was in online school, and I had to physically be present to oversee that; I felt comfortable speaking up to my direct manager because he is so supportive of me. He advocates for me and let me telework for an entire year to accommodate the childcare and school situation. This was not the first time that he stepped up for me, either; when my mother-in-law was dying of cancer, he gave me flexibility to provide care for her. Even though company leadership hasn't shown much support, my manager makes me feel like family is the number-one priority, and so I'm happy working there.

Evaluating Your Efforts to Create Sustainable Support

Throughout this book, I have talked about the importance of evaluation, including evaluating your company policies, resources, and benefits, and evaluating the effectiveness of your own communication style with working moms. Another key evaluation managers should undertake is determining whether working moms are comfortable asking for what they need. Do the moms feel safe to speak up on their own behalf? Here is my recommendation for a quick self-assessment as we close out this topic together. Ask yourself one simple question: When was the last time a working mother on your team approached you, unprompted, for support? Here are some possible answers and pathways forward:

1. *Never or not often.* Stop here. You might not quite be at the level of sustainable support where there is an open feedback loop of working-mom communication. Consider taking more initiative to reach out to the working moms on your team. Start a conversation, build connection and empathy, create safe spaces for moms to speak up. As we learned through stories and feedback from working moms in this book, it is rare that silence in a workplace means the moms are just doing fine without support. Silence usually means moms fear repercussion, stigma, or judgment.

2. *Regularly, but with awkwardness.* Do not despair! Awkward conversations about breastfeeding, mental health, or flexible scheduling do not mean your team member is feeling unsupported. Remember the myriad experiences new moms are going through; lack of sleep, possible mental health challenges, physical recovery, and a whole lot of anxiety about being back at work. Help put your working moms at ease by validating their experience coming to you, such as by saying, "I am so glad you brought this to my attention, and I would love to support you in this," or, "It was really good to touch base with you on this topic, and I hope you'll come back anytime you need support."

3. *Regularly and with ease.* Congratulations! You as a manager may have created sustainable support for working moms in your job place. I still say "may have" created because the ultimate grade comes from the moms themselves. Since you are regularly and easily talking with these mothers when they approach you about what they need, it's time to simply ask, "Are you feeling comfortable asking for support when you need it?" In this case, you'll have the answer you need.

So, how are you doing in supporting working moms? Are they getting the support they need? Do you have some follow-up work to do with the working moms on your teams? Can you leverage the great support moms feel on your team to help support other new parents and employees who need support?

The End (Goal)

It's clear: to be successful in a job market that has gone through significant shifts in workplace expectations, successful managers will see support to working moms as a necessary part of their management skills and toolkit. And it's not just the pandemic that spurred these changes. For the past hundred years, the demographics of women in the workforce have been in a state of change. In recent years, the change has been even more rapid, reaching a tipping point toward a larger percent of women than men in the workforce, higher-than-ever educational attainment for women, and generational shifts in expectations for work culture and family on the part of new parents.

Intentional support and good communication are necessary requirements of workplace culture and management practices to attract the most qualified jobseekers, who are statistically likely to be working moms now or someday soon. And with every step you take that support beyond the minimum to be more thoughtful, more intentional, with moms included in the design of programs, benefits, and support, you will gain a competitive edge as a manager and organization.

So what is that "one simple step for managers to support working moms for team success"? I think you probably know the answer now. The simple step you need to take is to talk to the working moms on your team and explicitly ask what they want and need. Communication and intentional conversations are the pathway to creating a successful workplace culture of support for moms on your teams. Policies, benefits, programs, services, and peer support will stem from those conversations and will be great tools for both you and the moms. As you go forward in your support efforts, keep in mind:

- Ask working mothers what kind of support they need, and then ask again and again.
- Develop and demonstrate empathy and make connections to your own personal life transitions, challenges, and joys.
- Think about timing and delivery of messages, resources, and expectations that honor what working mothers have told you they need help with.
- Keep in mind that every working mom, every employee, is unique, and this is why you must have conversations, not one-size-fits-all plans or resources.

- Enlist other managers, colleagues, peers, and leadership around you to help provide the support through creative programs and services that support working moms.
- Remember that the continuum of parenthood extends beyond the baby years. Support is a long-term investment in team success and also creates a supportive work environment for all parents on your team.
- Measure your effectiveness as a manager supporting working moms—again, by asking working moms how they are doing—and how *you* are doing in creating a sustainable level of support for working moms on your teams.

As I finished writing this book, I reached out to my network of working moms and asked them, "If you could tell the whole world one thing that managers should know about working moms, what would that be?" Not a single answer submitted was about a specific benefit or policy that they wished for. Every answer sent to me reflected a similar sentiment:

Ask us. Ask us what we need. Words matter, both in doing the asking and in how you frame your support for working mothers in your organization. Managers

make or break a working mom's ability to do their job
and stay in their job.

So, managers: go ask your mothers *today* how you can support them. They are ready to talk. If you listen to them, if you support them, they will move mountains to do their best work for your team, just like they move mountains every day to provide the best life they can for their families.

ACKNOWLEDGMENTS

I have never done any of this alone. Starting a successful business. Writing a book. Parenting. I am grateful to be surrounded by inspiring people who have gone out of their way to support me and lend their expertise and life advice at every step.

Again, I dedicate this book to my family for their unending support; recently at an appointment, my daughter's provider asked, "What is it again that you do for work, Mrs. Wells?" My eight-year-old proudly replied, "She does a ton of jobs!" She's right—I'm always juggling, and a book is yet another ball in the air that my family so wonderfully accepted and helped me carry. Thank you.

A special thanks to my business mentor, Nancy Strojny, for believing in my big ideas from day one and helping me craft and execute a plan to make Sarah Wells Bags come true.

My deep appreciation goes out to my book coach, Suzette Mullen, a guiding light in navigating this enormous and fascinating process of becoming an author.

ACKNOWLEDGMENTS

I'm grateful to my dad, David Bollinger, for teaching me how to be a great storyteller with a mission; listening to you in the pulpit was perhaps the first time I realized there is an audience for the stories I need to tell.

Thank you to the "morning walking group" for absorbing endless amounts of chatter from me about the topics within this book before you'd even had your first cup of coffee. Your friendship has given me the confidence I needed to make this happen and means everything to me.

Thank you to Amanda Good for headshots that captured this moment so perfectly.

I am so grateful to my business team for cheering me on every step and for all the hard work you have and will put into making this book a success. You are all working mothers yourselves who inspire me every day.

And very importantly, thank you to all the working moms who have supported me over the years and who took my surveys, polls, and social media question boxes and emailed and direct messaged to make this book a reality.

It is my sincere honor and mission to tell your stories here.

224

ABOUT THE AUTHOR

 Sarah Wells is a respected voice in the realm of management, leadership, and the support of working mothers.

With a master's degree in public policy and women's studies from the George Washington University, complemented by a bachelor's degree in political science and women's studies from American University, Sarah brings a wealth of knowledge and advocacy to her work. Her contributions as a sought-after expert, workshop presenter, and podcast speaker in the domain of supporting working mothers' transitions back to work have made her an invaluable resource for employers and teams.

Sarah's leadership philosophy is characterized by an unwavering commitment to long-term, sustainable success for organizations. She believes in nurturing work environments that foster happiness and longevity among teams. Her career spans a decade at Women in Government, a national bipartisan association for state legislators, where she championed public policy initiatives aimed at empowering and educating women in elected office. Sarah's impact extended to her five-year tenure as the executive director of the National Consumer Voice for Quality Long-Term Care, an organization dedicated to representing the voices of individuals receiving care services in nursing homes, assisted living facilities, and at home. In both roles, she instigated transformative changes, introducing supportive employment policies, fostering team camaraderie, and implementing flexible work practices, resulting in substantial financial and performance improvements for these organizations.

In 2013, Sarah took her entrepreneurial spirit to new heights by founding Sarah Wells Breast Pump Bags, dedicated to empowering mothers with products that enhance their sense of dignity and functionality while transporting breast pumps to their workplace. A key contributor to her ongoing success is the exceptional relationship she maintains with her customers and her team, rooted in a profound commitment to supporting working mothers as they navigate their return-to-work journey.

Sarah's distinct vantage point, having occupied various roles as a manager and a working mother, coupled with her passion for both organizations and mothers, is underpinned by her direct access to valuable data gleaned from her business customer relationships that culminates in this book.

Interested in bringing Sarah in to speak? Or, want more ideas for awesome communication with moms?

Sarah offers speaking engagements, article and interview contributions, consultation, and other collaborations. Learn more at her website at goaskyourmothers.com.

Follow on social media:

@goaskyourmothers

@sarahwellsbags

linkedin.com/in/sarah-wells-author